# Growing as a Christian 101

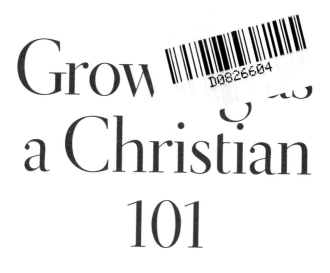

*Bruce* BICKEL
*&*
*Stan* JANTZ

HARVEST HOUSE™ PUBLISHERS

EUGENE, OREGON

*Cover design by Left Coast Design, Portland, Oregon*

*Cover illustration © Krieg Barrie Illustration*

**GROWING AS A CHRISTIAN 101**
Copyright © 2005 by Bruce Bickel and Stan Jantz
Published by Harvest House Publishers
Eugene, Oregon 97402
www.harvesthousepublishers.com

Library of Congress Cataloging-in-Publication Data
Bickel, Bruce, 1952-
    Growing as a Christian 101 / Bruce Bickel and Stan Jantz.
        p. cm. – (Christianity 101)
    Includes index.
    ISBN 0-7369-1431-5 (pbk.)
    1. Spiritual formation. 2. Spiritual life—Christianity. 3. Christian life. I. Jantz, Stan, 1952-
II. Title. III. Series.
    BV4511.B53 2004
    248.4—dc22

**Printed in the United States of America**

05   06   07   08   09   10   11   12   / BP-KB /   10   9   8   7   6   5   4   3   2   1

# Contents

# A Note from the Authors

Being a Christian requires balance. It involves both knowing about God (an intellectual component) and living in a manner that reflects Christlike qualities in your life (a behavioral component). The combination is critical. As a Christian, you want to live in a way that pleases God. But that requires knowledge of who God is. Correct thinking about God is the foundation of correct living for God.

We've previously written a book called *Knowing God 101* that focuses on the doctrines (beliefs) of Christianity. The book you currently hold in your hands is on the disciplines (behaviors) of the Christian life. But don't let that word *disciplines* mislead you. We're not referring to corrective punishment (like plagues of locusts or boils) for breaking the rules of acceptable Christian behavior. Nope, we're using *discipline* in a good sense, like when an athlete sticks with a training discipline until he or she wins an Olympic medal. After all, that's what Christian living is all about—a training program that moves us to the goal of reflecting the nature and character of Christ. Here's how the apostle Paul said it:

> But I keep working toward that day when I will finally be all that Christ Jesus saved me for and wants me to be. No, dear brothers and sisters, I am still not all I should be, but I am focusing all my energies on this one thing: Forgetting the past and looking forward to what lies ahead, I strain to reach the end of the race and receive the prize for which God, through Christ Jesus, is calling us up to heaven (Philippians 3:12-14).

This book is intended to help you reach that prize of knowing Christ better. Living the Christian life is the greatest adventure in the world. We are praying for you as you grow in your knowledge of Christ and in your personal relationship with Him.

# Introduction

*I*magine that you've won a magazine publisher's sweepstakes contest. (Come on, admit it. You've been praying that you'd win, even though you never subscribed to any of the magazines.) And suppose that your prize was a beautiful luxury yacht, equipped for sailing the high seas. As you step aboard that exquisite vessel for its maiden voyage to the Hawaiian Islands, you can hardly contain your excitement. You are exhilarated by the sound of the wind catching the sails, and you are ecstatic as you feel the sea mist blow against your face when your yacht pulls away from the pier and into the open sea. Ah, your high-seas adventure is underway.

But then your stomach drops and your knees weaken. Your face turns green and you lunge for the rail because you feel the sudden urge to hurl. This adverse reaction isn't the onset of seasickness. It is your shocking realization that you are on the boat alone. You have no captain, no crew. And you've never sailed before and have absolutely no idea what to do. What you expected to be a tranquil sail to paradise has turned out to be filled with panic and uncertainty. You are totally overwhelmed and intimidated by your new circumstances.

And so it is for many people who begin their Christian experience. They experience indescribable peace and excitement the moment they connect in a personal way with Jesus Christ. They eagerly anticipate the spiritual journey on which they are about to embark. But they might soon become overwhelmed by the significance and enormity of what has happened. They are living in a new dimension—a spiritual one—that is totally foreign to them. Other people are willing to be of assistance, but they often use terminology and jargon that is confusing. A new Christian can easily be intimidated by all the unknown, and going to a church doesn't help someone who might feel awkward, conspicuous, and unfamiliar with the apparent code of conduct.

If you are a Christian, you are on a spiritual journey of knowing God better and becoming more like Christ. It is a continual growth process. No one reaches full maturity as a Christian while on earth, so don't be distressed if you are a brand-new Christian and unfamiliar with the developmental dynamics. You are to be congratulated that you are learning how you go about growing in your faith. The basics are relatively simple to understand, and you'll soon see God's grand design for your spiritual growth. When you're on track in your spiritual life, you'll still be overwhelmed, not by uncertainty or intimidation but by the love of Christ and the sense of His presence in your life.

## What You'll Find Inside

The purpose of this book is to provide an overview of the essential building blocks for growing in the Christian faith. We'll familiarize you with the key components of God's plan for your spiritual development. Along the way, you'll find some pretty interesting information:

- *Answers to big questions:* How do I find God's will for my life? What role does the Holy Spirit play in my life? How do I hear God speak to me? How can I know which church I should attend?

- *Answers to small questions:* Which kind of Bible should I use? Do I need to read the Bible every day (and if so, what is the time limit)? What does *amen* mean? Can I bring my own snack instead of what the church serves for Communion?

- *Answers to questions you might be afraid to ask anyone else:* When that container is passed down my row during "offering" time, am I supposed to put something in or can I take something out? Why is raising my hand acceptable during a worship song but not if I have a question during the sermon?

## Why You Need to Read This Book

This may come as a surprise to you: God never intended that you would live the Christian life all by yourself, without any help from others. And that is precisely why God made some resources available to you:

- the example of Jesus Christ,
- the Holy Spirit,
- the Bible, and
- other Christians.

If you try to live the Christian life on your own, you'll be doomed for failure and frustration. But if you tap into the resources and guidance that God has waiting for you, your Christian life will be supercharged. Literally. God will be at work in you with full force.

The discussion in this book is introductory, but it presents God's design for spiritual growth, which should continue throughout your life. You can easily be detoured from the path of knowing God better if you stop making forward progress. If you ignore any of the components of God's plan for spiritual growth, your development will be stunted. Your spiritual life will become dry and boring. Don't settle for a mediocre spiritual existence. Don't get mired in Christian complacency. Learn what you need to do to grow in your faith, and then commit yourself to the process.

## This Book Is for You If...

Between the two of us, we have more than a few decades of Christian experience. We know what being a new Christian is like, and we also know about being a longtime Christian in search of a more passionate relationship with Christ. With that perspective in mind, we think you'll find this book on spiritual growth to be helpful if you're in any of the following categories:

- You just became a Christian, and now you're wondering what comes next.

- You're feeling a little guilty about your lack of progress as a Christian. You seem to be taking one step forward and two steps back. You could use some help in making your Christian life more consistent.

- You've been a Christian for a while, but things aren't clicking in your spiritual life right now. You know Jesus promised an abundant life (John 10:10), but you just aren't feeling it.

- You grew up in a Christian environment that seemed oppressive and legalistic, so you abandoned it years ago. Now you're interested in connecting (or reconnecting) with Christ, but you're looking for a relationship rather than regulations.

- You bristle at the suggestion of a formula for being a better Christian. Hey, we aren't dealing with a weight-loss gimmick here, so let's dispense with anything that smacks of "just 15 minutes a day," or "five easy steps," or a 30-day program.

## How to Use This Book

You aren't required to begin reading at page 1 and plow straight through until you hit the back cover. This book covers different subjects, and the respective discussions are relatively independent from the preceding chapters. Of course, we think a discussion of growing as a Christian has a logical flow, so we're partial to the arrangement of the chapters we've used. But if you've got a burning question on a hot topic and don't want to wait, you've got our permission to skip ahead. (You can use the table of contents or the index to get you where you can't wait to go.)

Some other features of this book might facilitate your study:

1. *Questions for Reflection and Discussion.* At the end of every chapter, we've included questions designed to help you personally apply the concepts to your own Christian experience.

2. *Online resources.* To the extent that a book can be interactive, this one is. An online resource is available for readers of *Growing as a Christian 101* and the other books and Bible studies in the Christianity 101 series. Check out the website at www.christianity101online.com. There you will find more commentary and additional questions. You can also send us your questions and comments. See page 271 for a more detailed explanation of features of the website.

3. *Dig Deeper.* At the end of every chapter, we've included a list of some of the books that we used in our research. We heartily recommend these books to you if you want to know more about the subject of that particular chapter.

## A Final Comment Before You Begin

Growing in the Christian life is an adventure, but it isn't always easy. It takes discipline, commitment, and perseverance. Without a doubt, the rewards are worth the effort. Here is how the apostle Paul explained it:

*I pray that from his glorious, unlimited resources [God] will give you mighty inner strength through his Holy Spirit. And I pray that Christ will be more and more at home in your hearts as you trust in him. May your roots go down deep into the soil of God's marvelous love. And may you have the power to understand, as all God's people should, how wide, how long, how high, and how deep his love really is. May you experience the love of Christ, though it is so great you will never fully understand it. Then you will be filled with the fullness of life and power that comes from God* (Ephesians 3:16-19).

May that be your motivation as you seek to grow in your Christian life.

# Chapter 1

Christianity is not primarily a theological
system, an ethical system, a ritual system, a
social system, or an ecclesiastical system—it
is a person: it's Jesus Christ, and to be a
Christian is to know Him and follow Him
and believe in Him.

*John R.W. Stott*

We're going to let you in on a little secret: Your Christian life is all about Jesus. Even your name—*Christian*—is a clue to who you are. You are in Christ! Before you became a Christian, you probably thought of Jesus as just another human being—a great human being, but merely human nonetheless. But now that Jesus has saved you by His life, His death, and His resurrection, you are a completely new person—a Christian. To paraphrase the apostle Paul, you're not the same anymore, for your old life is gone and your new life has begun (2 Corinthians 5:17). And it's all because of Jesus.

In this first chapter we're going to take a close look at the person and work of Jesus Christ. If you want to grow as a Christian, you're going to want to know who Jesus is and what He did for you.

# Jesus:
# The Reason
# You're a Christian

## *W*hat's *A*head

- ☐ Who Was Jesus?
- ☐ The Deity of Jesus
- ☐ The Humanity of Jesus
- ☐ Why Did Jesus Have to Die?
- ☐ The Resurrection of Jesus
- ☐ Where Is Jesus Now?

*N*o other person in the history of the world is as famous as Jesus. The majority of the six billion people living on earth right now know the name of Jesus, and at least one-third of all people—more than two billion—identify with Jesus Christ by calling themselves Christians. Yet what do we know about the life of this person who called Himself the Son of God? Did Jesus really do everything the Bible says He did? Did He actually heal the sick, raise the dead, calm the seas, die on a cross, and come back to life again? How do we know it's all true? And if it's true, what difference does it make?

It makes a big difference, because if you don't have confidence that Jesus did these things, then you aren't going to grow as a Christian. Your Christian life is built on the Good News that Jesus lived a perfect life, that He died for your sins, that He was buried, and that He was raised from the dead on the third day, just as the Bible says (1 Corinthians 15:1-4). These events aren't part of a myth or a nice story you have to believe by blind faith. These are things you can actually *know*. Your faith is based on things that actually happened.

As we explore the life and work of Jesus, we're going to start by looking at historical Jesus through the eyes of those who knew Him. Then we will look at His unique God-man nature and His central reason for coming into this world—to seek and to save those who are lost (Luke 19:10). Finally, we will evaluate the resurrection of Jesus, the remarkable historical event your Christian life depends on.

## Who Was Jesus?

To get to the heart of the historical Jesus, we need to find out what His contemporaries thought and wrote about Him. These eyewitness accounts tell us a great deal about who Jesus was and what He did.

### The Disciples

The people who knew Jesus best were His disciples, hand-picked by Jesus (the word *disciple* means "learner" or "follower"). All but one of these 12 ordinary men followed Jesus wholeheartedly. Jesus recruited "the Twelve" after His baptism, which marked the beginning of His public ministry. For the next three years—up until the time He ascended into heaven—Jesus taught this ragtag group, and gradually they learned. More importantly, they came to believe in Him as their Savior.

Two of Jesus' disciples, Matthew and John, were also biographers of Jesus. They and two other biographers wrote the four Gospels. Craig Blomberg, one of the most respected authorities on the biographies of Jesus, has this to say about their credibility:

> In terms of honesty, in terms of truthfulness, in terms of virtue and morality, these people [the biographers] had a track record that should be envied.

## The Opposition

If anyone had reason to discredit Jesus, it was the people who opposed Him, such as the religious leaders. If anyone had any doubts that Jesus spoke with authority, or that His followers accurately communicated His claims, the religious leaders would have jumped on the opportunity to expose Jesus as a fraud. But that never happened. No one ever contradicted the claims and teachings of Jesus. No one ever successfully argued with Jesus and proved Him wrong. His enemies could only silence Jesus by putting Him to death, which actually served to validate the prophecies concerning the Messiah and accomplish what Jesus came to do.

## The Historians

Even though the Bible is the most reliable and trustworthy ancient document ever written, some people want more evidence for the existence of Jesus. "Show me something other than the Bible that says Jesus lived and walked the earth in first-century Palestine," someone might ask you. Here's how you can respond. Josephus was a Jewish historian who lived and wrote in the first century. His writings, which are respected by scholars as trustworthy, mention Jesus several times. Other ancient secular writers—including Cornelius Tacitus and Plinius Secundus—made references to Christ, Christians, and historic events mentioned in the Bible. For example, the first-century historian Phlegon wrote about the darkness that came upon the earth at the time of Christ's crucifixion.

# The Deity of Jesus

One thing separates Jesus from every other religious leader in history:

*He claimed to be God!*

He didn't say He was *like* a god. He said that He *was* God. When referring to God the Father, Jesus said bluntly, "The Father and I are one" (John 10:30). It's doubtful that Jesus made this bold statement in jest or in a desperate attempt to get attention. He said it because it was true. The religious leaders certainly knew what Jesus meant, and they plotted His death because of His claim (John 5:18).

Jesus wasn't the only one who believed that He was God. John the Baptist recognized the deity of Christ (John 1:29), and the apostle Paul wrote this about Jesus: "For in Christ the fullness of God lives in a human body" (Colossians 2:9). This single distinction—the claim of Jesus to be God—is the foundation of Christianity. And we can believe it for at least three reasons: Jesus had the proof to back up His claim, He fulfilled Old Testament prophecy to the letter, and He had His Father's endorsement.

---

## *I*ncarnation and the Deity of Christ

Although you won't find it in the Bible, the church has used the word *incarnation* to refer to the fact that Jesus was God in human flesh. Wayne Grudem writes, "The *incarnation* was the act of God the Son whereby he took to himself a human nature."

---

### *Jesus Had the Proof to Back Up His Claim*

Jesus not only claimed to be God, He also played the part. He assumed the role that only God could fill when He forgave people of their sins. One day He was preaching in a house to a standing-room-only crowd when several men lowered their paralyzed friend down through the roof to be healed by Jesus (Mark 2:1-12). The first thing Jesus did was to tell the man, "My son, your sins are forgiven." Some religious leaders who were in the house were outraged. "This is blasphemy!" they exclaimed. "Who but God can forgive sins!"

We know what you might be thinking: *Claiming to possess the power to forgive sins doesn't prove that Jesus was God. Anyone can say that he is forgiving sins.* We agree. That's a good objection, except that Jesus then healed the paralyzed man, showing that He had supernatural powers that only God possesses. The healing of the paralyzed man wasn't a fluke. Jesus consistently exhibited supernatural powers that could only belong to God:

- He gave sight to the blind (Mark 8:22-26).

- He cured the lame (John 5:1-9).

- He healed the sick (Luke 7:1-10).

- He raised the dead to life (Matthew 9:18-26).

- He fed thousands with only a boy's lunch (Matthew 14:14-21).

- He calmed a raging storm with one command (Matthew 8:23-27).

Besides having these supernatural powers, Jesus had supernatural qualities that only God can possess:

- eternal (John 17:5)

- all-knowing (John 16:30)

- all-powerful (John 5:19)

- unchangeable (Hebrews 13:8)

- the Creator of the universe (Colossians 1:16)

## Jesus Fulfilled Prophecy Concerning the Messiah

Throughout the Old Testament, God promised the Jews that He would send a king who would establish God's kingdom on earth. This deliverer was referred to as the Messiah. He would be God Himself on earth. A big mystery surrounded the Messiah. Although the Jews knew He was coming (because God had promised), they weren't sure how they would know who He was, and they didn't know when He would arrive. But through the predictions in the Old Testament (called "prophecies" because the "prophets" announced them), the Jews had some fairly specific clues about this Messiah guy. Here is a portion of the checklist they were working from:

- *City of birth.* He was going to be born in the little town of Bethlehem (Micah 5:2).

- *Parentage.* He would be a direct descendant of the famous King David (Isaiah 11:1).

- *Distinguishing characteristics.* As strange as it seems, the Messiah would be born to a virgin (Isaiah 7:14). How inconceivable!

- *Childhood.* Although born in Bethlehem, He would spend His childhood in Egypt (Hosea 11:1).

- *Notoriety.* He would have a ceremonial entrance into Jerusalem on a donkey (Zechariah 9:9). A rather humble and inauspicious ceremony for a Messiah, don't you think?

- *Death.* He would die by crucifixion, the method of death reserved for the most heinous criminals (Psalm 34:20).

- *Famous last words.* Even the Messiah's last, dying words were predicted (Psalm 22:1).

- *Resurrection from the dead.* As if the "born of a virgin" thing were not enough, the Messiah was predicted to come back to life after His death (Psalm 16:9-10).

Over the centuries before Christ, as the list of prophecies about the Messiah became longer, the pool of potential candidates got smaller. That doesn't mean that the Jews didn't have their share of Messiah impostors. Similar to Elvis impersonators, the counterfeits were easy to spot. Oh, maybe they could fake a few of the criteria (by forging a birth certificate to show Bethlehem or riding a donkey into Jerusalem, for example), but the impostors weren't willing to be crucified, and none of them could pull off the "come back to life after death" prediction. But along came Jesus Christ. He claimed to be the long-awaited Messiah. And He had the résumé to back it up:

- born in Bethlehem (Luke 2:4-7)
- a descendant of King David (Luke 1:31-33)

- born of a virgin—which was very hard to fake (Matthew 1:18,22-23)

- raised in Egypt (Matthew 2:13-21)

- rode into Jerusalem on a donkey—the Palm Sunday parade (Matthew 21:2-5)

- famous last words (Mark 15:34)

- died on a cross (Matthew 27:32-35)

- came back to life—perhaps the hardest to fake (John 20–21)

No person before or after Christ has been able to pass the Messiahship test—only Christ.

### Jesus Had the Endorsement of God the Father

With a booming voice from heaven, God the Father announced that Jesus was His Son when Jesus was baptized by John the Baptist.

> *After his baptism, as Jesus came up out of the water, the heavens were opened and he saw the Spirit of God descending like a dove and settling on him. And a voice from heaven said, "This is my beloved Son, and I am fully pleased with him"* (Matthew 3:16-17).

This scene is amazing for two reasons:

- First, it reveals the three Persons of the Trinity present in one place at one time, distinct yet united: God the Father's voice is heard, Jesus Christ the Son is being baptized, and the Holy Spirit appears in the form of a dove.

- Secondly, and most pertinent to our discussion, God the Father is identifying Jesus as His Son. You can't get a better endorsement than from God Himself.

# The Mystery of the Three-in-One

Please excuse us if our discussion of Jesus being God and the Son of God seems a little confusing. It isn't our fault. Any discussion on this topic involves the mysterious concept of the Trinity— the three-in-one nature of God. The word Trinity doesn't even appear in the Bible, but it is an important aspect about God. The Trinity refers to the three distinct Persons who make up God:

- God the Father,
- Jesus Christ the Son, and
- the Holy Spirit.

The Trinity is not three gods who exist together to make up one God. There is only one God, but within that unity are three eternal and coequal Persons—all sharing the same essence and substance, but each one having a distinct existence.

## The Humanity of Jesus

Even though Jesus declared Himself to be God, the Bible describes Jesus Christ being all man. In fact, Jesus referred to Himself as "the Son of Man" (Luke 19:10). He frequently used this phrase in reference to Himself because He saw Himself as the representative for the human race. He identified Himself as being human. Jesus also identified His ancestry as human. He referred to Himself as the son of David because He was born into the bloodline of Israel's famous king. But the greatest evidence of His humanity is not what He said about Himself. His humanity is revealed in His life. Jesus Christ had traits that proved His humanity. Most significant of all, He had a body. This is obvious because so many people saw Him and touched Him. No one could have nailed a spirit to the cross. And His body had all of the traits that come with a human body (and which don't belong to a spirit):

- Jesus got hungry (Matthew 4:2).

- Jesus got thirsty (John 19:28).

- Jesus grew weary (John 4:6).

- Jesus experienced human love and compassion (Matthew 9:36).

- Jesus cried (John 11:35).

- Jesus was tempted (Hebrews 4:15).

These are the characteristics of a human. If Jesus was only all God stuffed into human skin, He could have existed on earth as a type of cyborg in human form without human feelings. But that isn't how it was. He had all of the human emotions and was just like we are...except for one major difference.

### Everything About Him Was Human...Except for the Sin Part

Yes, Jesus was completely human, with one major—very major—distinction from the rest of us. He was sinless. That means that He never did anything that displeased God or violated the Mosaic Law. At every stage of His life (infancy, boyhood, adolescence, and manhood), He was holy and without sin.

Jesus must have considered Himself to be sinless. He was a Jew, and Jews customarily offered sacrifices for their sins. But we have no record of Jesus ever offering a single sacrifice, even though He was frequently in the temple. He didn't need to. He was without sin. Perhaps the best proof of His sinlessness was demonstrated at the trials preceding His crucifixion. The religious authorities would have loved to present evidence that He had broken a law—religious or civil—but He hadn't. He was declared innocent 11 times:

- six times by Pilate (Matthew 27:24; Luke 23:14,22; John 18:38; 19:4,6)

- once by Herod (Luke 23:15)

- once by Pilate's wife (Matthew 27:19)

- once by the repentant thief (Luke 23:41)

- once by a Roman centurion (Matthew 27:54)
- once by Judas (Matthew 27:4)

The Bible offers further reliable proof that Jesus was without sin: He died for our sins. He could only be an acceptable sacrifice if He was sinless. All of Christianity is premised on that fact. The disciples—who knew Christ better than anyone—would not have been willing to be persecuted for their faith if they knew Christ was guilty of sin and if Christianity was based on a faulty premise. But these disciples declared Christ's holiness. Peter said it plainly: "He [Jesus] never sinned" (1 Peter 2:22). The disciple John echoed the same truth: "And you know that Jesus came to take away our sins, for there is no sin in him" (1 John 3:5). And the apostle Paul summed it up this way: "For God made Christ, who never sinned, to be the offering for our sin, so that we could be made right with God through Christ" (2 Corinthians 5:21).

## Why Did Jesus Have to Die?

The reason Christ had to die was to win our salvation. As sinners, we deserve the penalty for sin, which is death (Romans 6:23). Because God is holy and just, He demands a punishment for sin. A penalty must be paid, and we aren't capable of paying the penalty because we are sinners. The only one who can offer an acceptable payment is Jesus because only He is without sin.

The Bible clearly tells us that love caused God to send Jesus to pay the penalty for our sin:

*This is real love. It is not that we loved God, but that he loved us and sent his Son as a sacrifice to take away our sins* (1 John 4:10).

The work that Christ did in His life and in His death to accomplish our salvation is called the *atonement*. The death of Jesus by crucifixion was the pivotal event that allowed sinful humankind to get back into a right relationship with the holy, almighty God. The crucifixion of Christ wasn't a tragedy. It wasn't a series of events gone out of control. It was the divinely designed plan of God. Here is an abbreviated list of some of the fundamental accomplishments achieved by Christ's death on the cross. Each one is a vital part of God's plan of salvation for humankind.

# Is Jesus God or Man...or Both?

We have shown evidence for both the deity and the humanity of Christ. But how do these two natures—the divine and the human—come together in one person? Is Jesus all God, all man, or both? The answer is yes—to all three options. From our human perspective, this is a difficult concept to grasp, but it is not impossible or illogical. The person of Christ contains the union of His divine and human natures in one being. Jesus is all God and all man at the same time. When Jesus lived on earth, He demonstrated an interesting balance:

- *His deity wasn't limited by His humanity.* He was always God, as evidenced by His sinlessness and supernatural powers.

- *His humanity wasn't overshadowed by His deity.* Jesus didn't use His God powers to make His life easier. He experienced all the emotions we have. He even endured the pain and suffering of the cross. Jesus didn't give up His godly attributes. He simply took on human attributes as well (Philippians 2:6-7).

In His earthly body, Jesus voluntarily chose not to use all His godly powers. When He was hungry, He didn't turn the stones into bread. But He could have. When He was crucified, He didn't call down angels to rescue Him. But He could have. Choosing not to use an ability is different from not having it. And Jesus had it all: all God and all man.

*1. Substitution.* Christ died so that we don't have to. This is what Christianity is all about, and it required the death of Christ on the cross. It boils down to three basic points:

- All humans are sinful (Romans 3:23).

- The penalty for our sin is eternal death (Romans 6:23).

- Jesus was the ultimate human sacrifice. He died in our place (Romans 8:3-4).

*2. Propitiation.* If you're like us, the word *propitiation* doesn't find its way into your everyday vocabulary. Theologians use it to explain that Christ's death on the cross turned God's wrath away from us. Because God is so holy, He hates sin and is radically opposed to it. As sinful beings, we are the objects of God's wrath. But Christ's death on the cross appeased God's wrath.

> *For God sent Jesus to take the punishment for our sins and to satisfy God's anger against us* (Romans 3:25).

*3. Reconciliation.* Humankind was alienated from God because of sin. That alienation was removed when Christ died on the cross. Reconciliation between God and humanity is now possible.

> *For since we were restored to friendship with God by the death of his Son while we were still his enemies, we will certainly be delivered from eternal punishment by his life. So now we can rejoice in our wonderful new relationship with God—all because of what our Lord Jesus Christ has done for us in making us friends of God* (Romans 5:10-11).

*4. Redemption.* Before Christ died on the cross, we were slaves to sin. We were in bondage. We couldn't escape sin's snare. Think of it as if Satan had kidnapped you and was holding you as a hostage. Your release was dependent upon someone paying a ransom. That's exactly what Christ did on the cross. He paid the ransom to *redeem* you (literally, to purchase you back) from the slave market of sin. The ransom price was high. It cost Christ His life (1 Peter 1:18-19).

5. *Destruction.* Satan was behind all of this sin stuff from the beginning. (Remember the serpent in the Garden of Eden?) Not only did Christ's death on the cross free us from Satan's bondage, it also demolished the power of Satan in the process (Hebrews 2:14-15).

6. *Perfection.* In the Old Testament times, the priest had to offer a sacrifice on behalf of the people each year (in a ceremony referred to as "the Day of Atonement"). When Christ died on the cross, His sacrifice was enough to cover the sins of all people—past, present, and future.

> *He came once for all time, at the end of the age, to remove the power of sin forever by his sacrificial death for us. And just as it is destined that each person dies only once and after that comes judgment, so also Christ died only once as a sacrifice to take away the sins of many people* (Hebrews 9:26-28).

Salvation comes from what Jesus did without any help from us. He did everything that was necessary. Nothing else is required of us but to accept what He did for us.

## *W*hat Does the Cross Say?

To God the cross says "enough" because God is satisfied. To humankind the cross says "forgiven" because we are. To Satan the cross says "shut up" because it puts God and us on the same side.

*Fred Sanders*

## The Resurrection of Jesus

The death of Jesus on the cross for you is central to your Christian life, but it is central to a larger story, one that includes the resurrection. Without the resurrection of Jesus, the cross would be meaningless, because without the resurrection, there would be...

- *No Messiah.* The true Messiah must fulfill every single prophecy, including the prophecies that the Messiah would die for the sins of the world (Isaiah 53:7-8) and that God would raise Him from the dead (Psalm 16:9-10). If Jesus did not come back to life after dying, then He wasn't the Messiah. And if Jesus wasn't the Messiah, then both Jews and Gentiles alike (any non-Jew is a Gentile) are still waiting for salvation.

- *No eternal life.* Jesus didn't just say that He would be resurrected. He also said that He would provide a resurrection for us:

  *I am the resurrection and the life. Those who believe in me, even though they die like everyone else, will live again. They are given eternal life for believing in me and will never perish* (John 11:25-26).

  If Jesus wasn't raised from the dead, then Jesus was a big fat liar, and we have no hope for eternal life.

- *No heaven.* Do you think about heaven? We human beings can have no loftier thought. Now think about this: Without the resurrection of Jesus from the dead, we'll never get there. Jesus made it very clear that He is our connection to heaven. Not only is He designing and building a place in heaven for all who believe in Him, but He has also promised to take us there personally (John 14:1-4). As wonderful and amazing as heaven sounds, it doesn't mean a thing if Jesus is still dead.

- *No hope.* The bottom line is that without the resurrection, we're sunk. Oh yeah, we can appreciate the teachings of Jesus, we can do our best to imitate the life of Jesus, and we can feel good about living good lives here on earth. But what good is that if we don't have any hope of a life with Jesus beyond this one? If Christians are merely putting their faith in a dead guy, then they are just what Ted Turner once called them—a bunch of losers. Or as the apostle Paul put it:

> *If we have hope in Christ only for this life, we are the most miserable people in the world* (1 Corinthians 15:19).

## Did the Resurrection Really Happen?

The resurrection is so important to your faith that you need to know without a shadow of a doubt that it happened just as the Bible said. Yes, you can take God's Word for it, but you can also investigate the facts for yourself and see that they support what the Bible says. That way, if you are ever asked about your Christian hope (and we hope that you are), you will be ready to explain it (1 Peter 3:15).

Here are three proofs for the resurrection of Jesus Christ.

## 1. The Proof of the Empty Tomb

Ever since the resurrection, people who oppose Christianity have disputed the empty tomb. Here's the reasoning: If you disprove the resurrection by showing that the tomb wasn't really empty—or that it was empty for a reason other than the resurrection—then you can discredit Christianity. We don't disagree. So let's look at the three most popular explanations for the empty tomb (other than the resurrection) and see if they hold water.

*Explanation 1: Jesus didn't really die.* Some people believe that Jesus merely "swooned" from the torture, pain, and exhaustion of the crucifixion and then was buried alive. After three days, He was revived by the cool air of the tomb and walked out under His own power. Of course, if you believe that, then you believe that Jesus not only survived the crucifixion but also extricated Himself from 70 pounds of tightly wound grave clothes, knocked down a 1000-pound rock, and overpowered a bunch of armed Roman guards—all without the benefit of food and water for three days.

# Jesus Can't Lie

Max Anders adds one more objection to this theory. "If Jesus had somehow recovered from a deathlike swoon, He would have been a liar." This would have been completely inconsistent with His character. "Would a person of the integrity revealed in the Gospels have encouraged His followers to preach and base their lives on a lie?"

Besides, Jesus is God, and God cannot lie (Titus 1:2).

*Explanation 2: The disciples stole the body.* This theory was first proposed by the religious leaders (the very same ones who ordered the crucifixion). Knowing that the resurrection would ignite the Christian movement, they bribed the Roman soldiers assigned to guard the tomb to spread the rumor that the disciples stole the body of Jesus (Matthew 28:12-15). This theory is weak for a couple of reasons. First, it's unlikely that the religious leaders could have convinced all the guards to go along with their little scheme. Second, some of the guards would have certainly noticed the commotion caused by the disciples trying to pry back a huge stone and steal a corpse.

Even if the disciples were able to pull off this amazing feat of strength and daring, why would they die for a lie? Paul Little writes, "Each of the disciples faced the test of torture and martyrdom for his statements and beliefs. People will die for what they *believe* to be true, though it may actually be false. They do not, however, die for what they know is a lie."

*Explanation 3: The disciples were hallucinating.* They wanted so much to believe that Jesus was alive that they saw something (or someone) that wasn't really there. This theory has a couple of problems. First of all, the disciples weren't expecting Jesus to rise from the dead. In fact, when reports of the resurrection first came to the disciples, they didn't believe them (Mark 16:11). Second, the same hallucination could not possibly occur to hundreds of people in several locations over a period of 40 days. If anything, such a consistent report from that many people is a proof for the resurrection, not a refutation.

### 2. The Proof of Hundreds of Eyewitnesses

Jesus obviously wanted people to see Him after His resurrection, and hundreds did. The Bible records ten different appearances from the time He rose from the dead until His ascension into heaven 40 days later. He appeared to individuals (such as Mary Magdalene—see John 20:11-18), He appeared to two men walking to Emmaus (Luke 24:13-32), He appeared to the disciples, who couldn't believe their eyes (Luke 24:35-43), and He appeared to more than 500 people at one time (1 Corinthians 15:6).

### 3. The Proof of Transformed Believers

Once Jesus convinced the disciples that He wasn't a ghost, that He was alive, and that He was going to heaven to prepare a place for them, they went from being frightened to fearless. This is what happens when the living Jesus truly gets ahold of ordinary people, and it's one of the major proofs of the resurrection. The book of Acts tells the dramatic story of these transformed disciples. The Holy Spirit came upon them in power as Jesus promised (Acts 1:8), and they proclaimed the message that Jesus was alive. The power of the resurrection didn't stop with just those who saw Jesus for themselves. In the 2000 years since, it has provided the power to change lives.

## Where Is Jesus Now?

Jesus is in heaven now, "in the place of honor next to God, and all the angels and authorities and powers are bowing before him" (1 Peter 3:22). Does this mean Jesus is no longer here on earth with us? Not in body, but He is here spiritually, living in all who have invited Him into their lives (Colossians 1:27).

### What Is Jesus Doing?

Just because Jesus is at the right hand of God doesn't mean He is sitting around, biding His time until He returns to earth in the second coming. Jesus is engaged in at least three different very important activities, all of which concern you:

- *Jesus is preparing a place for you.* You can be sure that Jesus is engaged in the most spectacular construction project in the history of the universe: He's preparing heaven...for you (John 14:2).

- *Jesus is praying for you.* Actually, the Bible says that Jesus is "pleading" to the Father on your behalf (Romans 8:34). Who better to plead your case before God? No one knows you better than Jesus (Hebrews 4:15-16).

- *Jesus is keeping the universe going for you.* The universe functions so beautifully for a reason: Jesus is holding all creation together (Colossians 1:17).

### Jesus Is Coming Back

Jesus has promised to do one final thing, and that's to come to earth a second time (that's why they call it "the second coming"). Jesus said, "When everything is ready, I will come and get you, so that you will always be with me where I am" (John 14:3). This isn't a fairy tale. This is real. And it's the most exciting prospect you could ever have in life, made possible by the resurrection of Jesus Christ.

*Now we live with a wonderful expectation because Jesus Christ rose again from the dead* (1 Peter 1:3).

# What's That Again?

1. We know that Jesus was an actual historic person from the eyewitness accounts of His disciples (including those who wrote biographies about Jesus), His enemies, and Jewish and Roman historians.

2. The claim of Jesus to be God is the foundation of Christianity. Jesus had proof to back His claim: He forgave sins, had supernatural powers, and had supernatural qualities only God can possess.

3. Jesus fulfilled every prophecy concerning the Messiah. No other person before or after Christ has been able to pass the Messiahship test.

4. Even though Jesus was all God, He was also all human—but He was sinless.

5. Christ died to provide our salvation. The work He did to do this is called the *atonement,* and it involved substitution, propitiation, reconciliation, redemption, destruction, and perfection.

6. Without the resurrection of Jesus from the dead, His death on the cross would be meaningless.

7. The empty tomb is a historic fact that cannot be explained away.

8. Jesus is in heaven now preparing a place for us, praying for us, and keeping the universe going for us. And let's always remember that Jesus is also coming back for us.

## Dig Deeper

Here are our top recommendations for books about Jesus:

*More Than a Carpenter* by Josh McDowell is one of the most popular books about Jesus ever written. It's simple, concise, and compelling.

*The Case for Christ* is by Lee Strobel, a journalist and former atheist who investigated the evidence for Jesus.

*Jesus Christ Our Lord* by John Walvoord is a classic study on the Person and work of Christ.

Our own book, *Why Jesus Matters,* considers the eternal impact of Jesus Christ on history, culture, science, the arts, morality, and personal relationships.

# $Q$uestions for $R$eflection and $D$iscussion

1. Why is it important to know that Jesus is a real person whose existence is historically verifiable? Why is it just as important to know that Jesus had supernatural powers and qualities? Why is it unacceptable to strip Jesus of His supernatural powers and qualities?

2. As best you can, explain the difference between the biblical concept of the *Trinity* (three Persons in one God) and the unbiblical concept of *tritheism* (three gods that make up one God).

3. List three proofs that show Jesus lived a sinless life.

4. Explain how the deity of Jesus wasn't limited by His humanity. How was His humanity not overshadowed by His deity?

5. Write a one-sentence summary for each of these key doctrinal words:

- substitution
- propitiation
- reconciliation
- redemption
- destruction
- perfection

6. Read 1 Corinthians 15:12-19. Under what condition would Christians be the most miserable people in the world?

7. Which of the three proofs for the resurrection of Jesus gives you the most assurance? Why are all three proofs important?

## Moving On...

Just a few hours before Jesus was arrested and sentenced to death, He met with His disciples in the upper room. Jesus told the men who had been closest to Him that even though He would soon be leaving them, He would not be leaving them alone. "And I will ask the Father, and he will give you another Counselor, who will never leave you," Jesus said. "He is the Holy Spirit, who leads into all truth" (John 14:16-17).

Even though Jesus is now in heaven at the right hand of the Father, the Spirit of Christ—the Holy Spirit—is here with us. If you are a Christian, then Christ lives in you because the Holy Spirit indwells you, helping you to live the life that Jesus wants you to live. That's what we're going to talk about in the next chapter.

# Chapter 2

The word "Comforter" as applied to the
Holy Spirit needs to be translated by some
vigorous term. Literally, it means "with
strength." Jesus promised His followers that
"The Strengthener" would be with them forever. This promise is no lullaby for the faint-
hearted. It is a blood transfusion for
courageous living.

*E. Paul Hovey*

We know we're still near the beginning of this book, but it is time to be brutally honest. We wouldn't be doing you any favors to keep it a secret any longer. Maybe no one told you this when you became a Christian, but we'll give it to you straight and won't pull any punches. Here's the bad news: *You can't successfully grow as a Christian in your own strength.* You don't have what it takes. There are spiritual dynamics at play that make you ill-equipped and outclassed.

> *For we are not fighting against people made of flesh and blood, but against the evil rulers and authorities of the unseen world, against those mighty powers of darkness who rule this world, and against wicked spirits in the heavenly realms* (Ephesians 6:12).

You don't stand a chance on your own. But wait...don't despair. We have good news: Because you're a Christian, God lives in you and spiritually equips you with supernatural power to be victorious in your Christian life. Your internal source of spiritual power is the Holy Spirit.

This will be an exciting chapter for you. We'll be talking about what God's got going on inside of you.

# The Holy Spirit:
# Your Power Source

## *W*hat's *A*head

- ☐ The Initiator of Spiritual Transformation
- ☐ The Guide to Spiritual Understanding
- ☐ The Producer of Spiritual Fruit
- ☐ The Giver of Spiritual Gifts

*P*ut yourself in the place of the very first Christians ten days after Christ returned to heaven. They were probably feeling alone and abandoned. On the night before He was crucified, Jesus had promised the disciples that He would send the Holy Spirit to be with them, but that was seven weeks ago, and now they're beginning to wonder if the Holy Spirit came but they missed it. Not hardly. On the fiftieth day after the resurrection, the Holy Spirit came to earth with a spectacular arrival. The supernatural phenomenon that occurred is often referred to as Pentecost because it occurred on the Jewish holiday known as the Feast of Pentecost.

*T*he Jews celebrated the Feast of Pentecost to commemorate God giving the law to Moses. Bible scholars have said that the Holy Spirit's arrival on that day was no mere coincidence. The sacrifice of Christ on the cross replaced the law, so now we can celebrate God giving the Holy Spirit to us.

Here is the report of what happened that morning at Pentecost:

> *On the day of Pentecost, seven weeks after Jesus' resurrection, the believers were meeting together in one place. Suddenly, there was a sound from heaven like the roaring of a mighty windstorm in the skies above them, and it filled the house where they were meeting. Then, what looked like flames or tongues of fire appeared and settled on each of them. And everyone present was filled with the Holy Spirit and began speaking in other languages, as the Holy Spirit gave them this ability* (Acts 2:1-4).

Talk about making a grand entrance! The roar of wind, the appearance of fire, and speaking in different languages is enough to draw a large crowd of spectators, and that is exactly what happened. The crowd immediately realized that the believers weren't just spouting out a bunch of gibberish. The residents of Jerusalem who were immigrants from foreign countries recognized their native languages. This was all part of the divine plan to prove the supernatural existence of God and to spread the message that Jesus Christ is the way of salvation. How convenient that the Holy Spirit also provided the message in multiple languages so that nothing would be lost in the translation (Acts 2:5-11).

Although the disciple Peter had wimped out and denied Jesus on the evening before the crucifixion, the Holy Spirit made him bold on this occasion. He spoke directly to the crowd, who thought the disciples were drunk, and explained what was going on:

> *Then Peter stepped forward with the eleven other apostles and shouted to the crowd, "Listen carefully, all of you,*

*fellow Jews and residents of Jerusalem! Make no mistake
about this. Some of you are saying these people are drunk.
It isn't true! It's much too early for that. People don't get
drunk by nine o'clock in the morning"* (Acts 2:14-15).

Peter went on to explain that this miracle was another step in
God's progressive plan to reveal that salvation is available to the
people of the world through Jesus Christ. The sight of flames, the
sounds of the foreign languages, and the sense of Peter's sermon
were enough to convince the crowd that a God thing was happening. They wanted to know how they should respond, so Peter
told them:

*Each of you must turn from your sins and turn to God, and
be baptized in the name of Jesus Christ for the forgiveness
of your sins. Then you will receive the gift of the Holy
Spirit. This promise is to you and to your children, and even
to the Gentiles—all who have been called by the Lord our
God* (Acts 2:38-39).

---

*D*on't think that Pentecost was some little Holy Roller church gath-
ering with a few bystanders who got caught up in the excitement and
the emotion. The Bible says that 3000 people believed what Peter
said (Acts 2:41).

---

The events of Pentecost mark the beginning of the Holy
Spirit's involvement in the lives of those who believe and follow
Christ. And the Holy Spirit has been at it ever since. Sometimes
you'll know—without a doubt—that He is working because the
results are supernatural. Other times He is a bit more inconspic-
uous (we doubt that you've seen a flame of fire over your head).
But all that He does, conspicuous or not, is spectacular. So that you
don't miss any aspect of His amazing activities, we'll review in this
chapter what the Holy Spirit accomplishes in your life.

# More to Know

The Holy Spirit wasn't snoozing through eternity until the time of Pentecost. He played an active role in the creation of the universe, and He was involved in the lives of many people in Old Testament times and in the life of Christ.

You should learn more about the Holy Spirit than just His role in helping you grow as a Christian. You should also know the "theology" of the Holy Spirit—that He, as a part of the Trinity, is God. You also need to understand that He is a Person and not just some impersonal force.

We aren't modest enough to refrain from suggesting *Knowing God 101* from this Christianity 101 series for more information about the doctrine of the Holy Spirit. Check out our chapter on the Trinity ("When Three Equals One") as well as the chapter on the Holy Spirit ("Much More than Just a Friendly Ghost").

## The Initiator of Spiritual Transformation

Anyone who has ever believed in Jesus as Savior has the Holy Spirit to thank. You can't take credit for it yourself because the Holy Spirit was the One who initiated the entire process. The Holy Spirit is the One who turns people's hearts and minds toward Christ. (See John 16:8-9.)

Without Christ, our lives are about as useless and powerless as trash. But through the energizing, recycling work of the Holy Spirit, you can be remade into something useful to God. It's the new and improved you! (See John 3:5-6.) The work of the Holy Spirit doesn't end when a person becomes a believer. That just marks the beginning of the Holy Spirit's transformation process.

### It's an Inside Job

The Holy Spirit actually lives inside each believer. Of course, the Holy Spirit won't show up on a CAT scan or in an X-ray, and you can't use Him as an excuse for that bloated feeling you've had recently. But if you are a follower of Christ, the Holy Spirit is present in your life.

This role of the Holy Spirit is referred to as His *indwelling*. (Even we can understand how the theologians came up with that term.) Think of it as if your body is a temple for the Holy Spirit. That is not our analogy—it's in the Bible.

> *Or don't you know that your body is the temple of the Holy Spirit, who lives in you and was given to you by God?* (1 Corinthians 6:19).

Think about these two significant consequences of the Holy Spirit indwelling your life:

1. You should be mindful that the Spirit of God lives within you. If you are doing things or going places that you shouldn't, you are dragging God along into that mess.

2. If you relinquish control of your life to God, He can help you avoid worldly temptations because His Spirit lives within you.

   > *But you are not controlled by your sinful nature. You are controlled by the Spirit if you have the Spirit of God living in you* (Romans 8:9).

### The Change Maker

Your spiritual relationship with God also requires a growing maturity. It is a process that happens over time. Everybody messes up every once in a while, but we should all be making progress.

The Holy Spirit is available to help you in the process of becoming spiritually mature. Here are some of the changes that we'll discuss in the rest of this chapter:

- He can give you spiritual insight and guide you in truth (John 16:12-15).

- He can assist you in praying according to the will of God (Romans 8:26; Ephesians 6:18).

- He produces God's character within you (Galatians 5:22-23).

- He empowers you with one or more spiritual gifts (1 Corinthians 12:7).

- He equips you for spiritual battle against temptation and the forces of Satan (Romans 8:13; Galatians 5:16-17).

When the process of spiritual transformation seems too slow, some people complain that they need to get more of the Holy Spirit in their life. They've got it all wrong. Spiritual maturity is never a question of getting more of the Holy Spirit. If you are a believer, you already have all of Him. The question is just the opposite: "How much *of you* does the Holy Spirit have?"

The apostle Paul knew that we would make progress in our spiritual maturity only when we make our entire lives available to the Holy Spirit. The more control we allow Him to have in our lives, the more Christlike we will become. The concept is referred to as "being filled with the Holy Spirit":

*Let the Holy Spirit fill and control you* (Ephesians 5:18).

The Holy Spirit indwells you for the purpose of making you more like Christ. But He's a perfect gentleman, and He won't force the changes to happen unless you are in agreement. You need to yield yourself to the control of the Holy Spirit, and then the "filling" will happen. Then be prepared to be amazed by the changes in your life.

## The Guide to Spiritual Understanding

When Jesus walked the earth, He was the world's greatest spiritual guide. On the night before He was crucified, He explained to His disciples that He would be returning to heaven, but He wouldn't abandon them. In His place, God was going to send the Holy Spirit:

> *I will ask the Father, and he will give you another Coun-*
> *selor, who will never leave you. He is the Holy Spirit*
> (John 14:16-17).

The name *counselor* is another word for guide. But a more descriptive word is *paraclete* (which is the Greek word used in John's Gospel). A paraclete is someone who comes alongside you as a companion to counsel, comfort, instruct, and advise you—everything a great spiritual guide should do. That was certainly an accurate description for the Holy Spirit, because He provides spiritual guidance to us in the following ways:

*1. The Holy Spirit helps you pray.*

Prayer is such an important activity for the Christian because it's the way you talk with God and tell Him your greatest needs and your deepest desires. It's how you ask God for direction. And yet how many times have you tried to pray, and you just didn't know what to say, or you prayed and you didn't feel like you were getting through to God. What do you do? That's where the Holy Spirit comes in. As your Helper, the Holy Spirit does something utterly amazing for you:

> *And the Holy Spirit helps us in our distress. For we don't*
> *even know what we should pray for, nor how we should*
> *pray. But the Holy Spirit prays for us with groanings that*
> *cannot be expressed in words. And the Father who knows*
> *all hearts knows what the Spirit is saying, for the Spirit*
> *pleads for us believers in harmony with God's own will*
> (Romans 8:26-27).

This is an amazing mystery. Even though you don't know what to pray for, as you pray the Holy Spirit tells God what is in your heart, and God knows exactly what He is saying because the Holy Spirit is in complete harmony with God.

The Holy Spirit not only prays for you but also tells you what to pray for:

*And continue to pray as you are directed by the Holy Spirit*
(Jude 20).

### 2. The Holy Spirit helps you love.

The Holy Spirit doesn't work with loners. When God saved you,
you were automatically baptized by the Holy Spirit into the
body of Christ so that you could serve and love other Christians
(1 Corinthians 12:13). In fact, our service and love for other
Christians proves to the world that we are followers of Christ
(John 13:35). If that seems tough to do sometimes, you can
thank God that He has given you the Holy Spirit to help you love
(1 John 4:11-13).

### 3. The Holy Spirit helps you worship.

God deserves all the praise and worship we can give Him, but
worshiping Him doesn't come naturally. We need help, and God
knows it. That's why He has given us the Holy Spirit to lead us into
worship (Philippians 3:3). Jesus told the Samaritan woman, "God
is Spirit, so those who worship him must worship in spirit and in
truth" (John 4:24). Whether you are in church worshiping with
other believers or you are alone in your quiet time, the Holy
Spirit will help you worship God in a way that pleases Him.

### 4. The Holy Spirit helps you in your stress.

Let's face it. Life is full of a lot of worry and stress. The Bible tells
us not to worry, but giving our concerns over to God can be
tough. We somehow think that if we hang on to our troubles, we
can solve them ourselves (but we seldom can). That's where the
Holy Spirit comes in. As your ultimate Comforter, the Holy Spirit
promises to console and assure you as you walk with the Lord (Acts
9:31). He promises to help you when you are mentally, physically,
or emotionally stressed (Romans 8:26).

The Holy Spirit also provides comfort by assuring you of your
salvation. At one time or another, you are going to wonder if you
are truly saved. Having doubts about your salvation is completely
normal, but that's not something you have to live with all the time.
Pray and ask God to comfort you through the Holy Spirit. Ask God
to assure you that you are saved, and He will do it.

*For His Holy Spirit speaks to us deep in our hearts and tells us that we are God's children* (Romans 8:16).

### 5. The Holy Spirit helps you in your decisions.

Do you want to know God's will for your life? Hey, we all do! But it doesn't come all at once. God's will is progressive and unfolds over time, kind of like a good mystery novel (except you can't skip ahead to see what's going to happen next). You have to take it one day at a time. As much as you would like to believe that God's will is about knowing the big stuff in life such as your career, your relationships, and your family, it's really more about walking daily with the Lord. And that's where the Holy Spirit comes in, guiding you step-by-step. He causes the big stuff to fall into place as you take consistent small steps in the right direction.

*If we are living now by the Holy Spirit, let us follow the Holy Spirit's leading in every part of our lives* (Galatians 5:25).

### 6. The Holy Spirit helps you comprehend God's truth.

The best (and easiest) way to learn what God wants you to know is to allow the Holy Spirit to be your Teacher. As part of the Trinity, the Holy Spirit knows the mind of God because the Holy Spirit is God. A primary role of the Holy Spirit is to help us understand God's way of thinking:

*No one can know God's thoughts except God's own Spirit. And God has actually given us his Spirit (not the world's spirit) so we can know the wonderful things God has freely given us* (1 Corinthians 2:11-12).

## The Producer of Spiritual Fruit

Another amazing work of the Holy Spirit involves producing godly character traits in your life. The Bible lists nine spiritual character qualities, known as "the fruit of the Spirit," that the Holy Spirit makes available to you. In his book *Secrets of the Vine*, Bruce Wilkinson writes this about the fruit of the Spirit:

In practical terms, fruit represents good works—a thought, attitude, or action of ours that God values because it glorifies Him. The fruit from your life is how God receives His due honor on earth. That's why Jesus declares, "By this My Father is glorified, that you bear much fruit" (John 15:8).

## A Different Perspective

Christians sometimes seem like fools to non-Christians. But anyone who doesn't have a personal relationship with God through Jesus Christ just doesn't get it. The smartest person in the world can't grasp the deep secrets of God. Here's why:

> But people who aren't Christians can't understand these truths from God's Spirit. It all sounds foolish to them because only those who have the Spirit can understand what the Spirit means. We who have the Spirit understand these things, but others can't understand us at all.... But we can understand these things, for we have the mind of Christ (1 Corinthians 2:14-16).

So don't be distressed when a pseudo-intellectual calls Christians a bunch of fools and losers, or some film producer portrays Christians as a bunch of raving lunatics. That's the only perspective they have because they are incapable of understanding the reality of God's truth.

Fruit and good works are mentioned several times in the Bible, but the most well-known verses are found in Galatians:

> But when the Holy Spirit controls our lives, he will produce this kind of fruit in us: love, joy, peace, patience, kindness, goodness, faithfulness, gentleness, and self-control (Galatians 5:22-23).

*T*he fruit of the Spirit are character qualities that God possesses and that the Holy Spirit imparts to us as we live in trusting obedience to Jesus.

In explaining the fruit of the Spirit, we'll follow Billy Graham's method of dividing these nine character qualities into three "clusters" of three fruit. Each cluster represents a different relationship in your life:

### Fruit Cluster 1: Love, Joy, and Peace—for Your "Godward" Relationship

The greatest of all Christian virtues is *love* (1 Corinthians 13:13), so this quality appropriately leads the list. First we are to love God. Jesus said, "You must love the Lord your God with all your heart, all your soul, and all your mind. This is the first and greatest commandment" (Matthew 22:37-38). Then we are to love our neighbor (Matthew 22:39) and other Christians (John 13:35). We are to model our love after God, who Himself is love (1 John 4:8). We should love with the same sacrificial love that motivated God to send Jesus into the world (John 3:16).

The world strives for happiness, but Christians should seek *joy*. The difference is that happiness depends on outward circumstances (like winning the lottery, having a baby, or watching your favorite sports team win a championship), whereas joy is based on obeying Jesus and knowing that He loves us. "I have told you this so that you will be filled with joy," Jesus said. "Yes, your joy will overflow!" (John 15:11). Joy isn't affected by the negative stuff that happens in your life. In fact, when you suffer—especially when you suffer for being a Christian—you can rejoice, "for then the glorious Spirit of God will come upon you" (1 Peter 4:14).

Everyone wants *peace*, but peace between people and nations is only temporary. In a world torn by strife, we need to show the peace of God, "which is far more wonderful than the human mind can understand" (Philippians 4:7). The peace that comes from the Holy Spirit will keep us united with our fellow Christians (Ephesians 4:3) and everyone else (Hebrews 12:14).

### Fruit Cluster 2: Patience, Kindness, and Goodness—for Your "Outward" Relationships

You don't develop *patience* when everything goes your way and people are doing what you want them to do. But when circumstances and people turn against you—that's when you need the kind of patience that only God can give you through the Holy Spirit.

> *We also pray that you will be strengthened with his glorious power so that you will have all the patience and endurance you need* (Colossians 1:11).

A few years ago someone wrote a little book called *Random Acts of Kindness*. Nothing is random about *spiritual kindness*. It includes deliberate acts of treating others with compassion (even if they are rude to you). To have this attitude means treating others the way God does. It means helping another Christian get "back onto the right path" (Galatians 6:1). It means that we "share each other's troubles and problems" (Galatians 6:2).

Sometimes you'll hear that someone did something out of the "goodness of his heart." That gets to the essence of *goodness*, which is closely related to kindness. When you help someone, not because he or she deserves it and not because you're looking for credit but simply because the Holy Spirit prompts you to—this is goodness.

### Fruit Cluster 3: Faithfulness, Gentleness, and Self-Control— for Your "Inward" Relationship

*Faithfulness* is different than faith. You exercise faith when you believe in God's plan to save you through Jesus (Ephesians 2:8), but the Holy Spirit produces the fruit of faithfulness in you when you let Him fill you. To be faithful means you are "entirely trustworthy and good" (Titus 2:10). If you are faithful, you are a person of your word as well as a person of God's Word.

Displaying the character trait of *gentleness* is not being wimpy. Jesus commended the gentle, "for the whole earth will belong to them" (Matthew 5:5). Billy Graham compares a gentle person to a wild horse that has been tamed. The power is still there, but it's under control. Dr. James Boice writes that gentle people "are always angry at the right time (such as against sin) and never angry at the wrong time."

The final characteristic is *self-control*, which enables you to have mastery over your thoughts and actions. If you have spiritual self-control, you let the Holy Spirit control your life (Galatians 5:22). Without self-control, you end up following "the desires of your sinful nature," and that's not a pretty sight (Galatians 5:19-21). In fact, the desires of the sinful nature are the "default setting" in everyone's life. To overcome what comes naturally, you need to make a choice every day and in every way to "live according to your new life in the Holy Spirit" (Galatians 5:16).

## The Giver of Spiritual Gifts

A spiritual gift is a God-given, supernatural ability to serve others. It may take the form of a special power of performance, or maybe knowledge, or sensitivity.

Most of the teaching in the Bible about spiritual gifts comes from the apostle Paul (but the apostle Peter sneaks in a little mention about them too). These are the gifts these different passages list:

- Romans 12:6-8—"God has given each of us the ability to do certain things well."

  | prophecy | encouragement | leadership |
  |----------|---------------|------------|
  | serving  | giving        | kindness   |
  | teaching |               |            |

- 1 Corinthians 12:4-11—"Now there are different kinds of spiritual gifts."

  | wisdom    | healing  | discernment    |
  |-----------|----------|----------------|
  | knowledge | miracles | tongues        |
  | faith     | prophecy | interpretation |

- Ephesians 4:11—"He is the one who gave these gifts to the church."

  | | | |
  |---|---|---|
  | apostle | evangelist | teacher |
  | prophet | pastor | |

- 1 Peter 4:10-11—"God has given gifts to each of you from this great variety of spiritual gifts. Manage them well so that God's generosity can flow through you."

  | | |
  |---|---|
  | speaking | service |

You may be anxious to know what your spiritual gift is, but before we see what these spiritual gifts look like, let's get a general sense of how they operate and what they are used for:

- The Holy Spirit distributes spiritual gifts as He chooses. He decides who gets what.

  *It is the one and only Holy Spirit who distributes these gifts. He alone decides which gift each person should have* (1 Corinthians 12:11).

- Every believer has at least one spiritual gift. No Christian is left out.

  *God has given gifts to each of you from his great variety of spiritual gifts* (1 Peter 4:10).

- A spiritual gift is given to each of us as a means of helping the entire Christian community (1 Corinthians 12:7). Your spiritual gift isn't given to you for your own personal enjoyment. Instead, you are supposed to use it to help other people.

- A spiritual gift does not have anything to do with a place. You don't have to use your gift only in a church building. Sure, the gift of serving may be used at the church property, but it is just as likely to be used in the homes of the people in the church and in your neighborhood.

- A spiritual gift is not a natural talent. The two may overlap, but a natural ability can be used for personal (or selfish) purposes, whereas a spiritual gift is designed, intended, and used to serve the Christian community.

## The Proof Is in the Power

The supernatural power of the spiritual gifts can be proof that God is involved in your life. Here is how the apostle Paul explained it to the Christians at Corinth:

*And my message and my preaching were very plain. I did not use wise and persuasive speeches, but the Holy Spirit was powerful among you. I did this so that you might trust the power of God rather than human wisdom* (1 Corinthians 2:4-5).

And he said it this way to the Christians in the city of Thessalonica:

*For when we brought you the Good News, it was not only with words but also with power, for the Holy Spirit gave you full assurance that what we said was true* (1 Thessalonians 1:5).

Other people may see God at work in your life through the spiritual gift that God has given to you. But more than anyone else, you will be impressed with God's presence and power in your life as you realize that things are happening that you couldn't do on your own.

### What Do I Do with It?

Bible scholars have spent considerable time and brainpower trying to analyze and compare the passages dealing with spiritual gifts. No one has a complete understanding of the biblical references, but several observations have been made:

1. All of the passages make reference to gifts of the Holy Spirit, but the basic orientation of each passage seems a little different. The verses from Ephesians suggest that these are roles within the church. The Romans and 1 Peter passages actually catalog several basic functions that are performed within the church. And the 1 Corinthians verses seem to be a list of special abilities. Because they have slightly different meanings in mind, no one should bust a gut trying to reduce the passages into a single, unified concept or definition of spiritual gifts.

2. *When* a person receives a spiritual gift is not clear. Since the Bible teaches that every believer has at least one, the predominant view is that a spiritual gift is received when a person becomes a Christian. If someone has multiple spiritual gifts, one may be given at the time of salvation, and another gift may be given later.

3. Since none of the four lists includes all of the gifts found in the other lists, they probably do not exhaust all the gifts of the Spirit. Individually and collectively, they might be representative (rather than exhaustive) of the type of supernatural empowerment that God gives to believers.

When you get to the bottom line of spiritual gifts, you only need to do two things:

1. Find out what your spiritual gift is; and

2. start using it.

In chapter 10 ("What to Do When You Go to Church"), we'll give you some specific examples of how these spiritual gifts work among God's family. For now, you just need to realize that God has equipped you with supernatural power for ministry and that the Holy Spirit is the source of that power within you.

## Let the Process Begin

No one said that living the Christian life was easy. (And if someone said that to you, they hadn't tried it correctly.) You will always struggle in a battle against your old sinful nature. But you don't have to struggle at the same level throughout your life. You can make progress toward a more mature and spiritual life—filled with power and passion for God—as you grow in your relationship with Christ. And you don't have to do it alone because the Holy Spirit is working inside you to make it happen as you yield control of your life to Him.

The Holy Spirit is in the ministry of sanctifying you. That means He wants to make you more holy in your life. To be sanctified literally means to be "set apart for service" to God. As Paul explains:

> There was a time when some of you were just like that, but now your sins have been washed away, and you have been set apart for God. You have been made right with God because of what the Lord Jesus Christ and the Spirit of our God have done for you (1 Corinthians 6:11).

When you became a Christian, two things happened. First, Jesus and the Holy Spirit washed your sins away. Second, the Holy Spirit began His work of sanctification in you. He set you apart for service to God. He is undertaking the lifelong process of making you holy as He develops the fruit of the Spirit in your life, and He is equipping you for service with a spiritual gift.

This process of sanctification continues until the day you die or until Jesus returns, whichever comes first. Only then will you be completely holy. Until that day, the Holy Spirit will be working in you toward this goal:

> We can be mirrors that brightly reflect the glory of the Lord. And as the Spirit of the Lord works within us, we become more and more like him and reflect his glory even more (2 Corinthians 3:18).

# What's That Again?

1. The only way to be truly spiritual is to allow the Holy Spirit to help you become spiritually minded in everything you do.

2. Jesus didn't abandon His followers when He returned to heaven. He sent the Holy Spirit as a spiritual Guide and Companion. The first occurrence of the Holy Spirit fulfilling this role was at an event known as Pentecost, where the power of the Holy Spirit was revealed by supernatural events.

3. The Holy Spirit is in the life of ("indwells") every believer. As believers, we are baptized into the body of Christ by the Holy Spirit, which means that we are united with God and united with all other believers. If we want to mature spiritually, we need to be filled by the Holy Spirit, which entails allowing Him to have control of our life.

4. The Holy Spirit indwells you to serve as your spiritual Helper, Counselor, Comforter, Guide, and Teacher. The Holy Spirit opens your mind to receive the truth of Scripture and to help you comprehend the nature and thoughts of God.

5. The Bible lists nine spiritual qualities known collectively as the fruit of the Spirit. These are character qualities that the Holy Spirit gives you as you live in obedience to Jesus.

6. Jesus promised that His followers would have supernatural power. That power is a "spiritual gift" from the Holy Spirit. Spiritual gifts are special abilities and sensitivities that benefit the Christian community. Every believer has at least one, and these gifts are distributed by the Holy Spirit to believers as He chooses.

## Dig Deeper

We're sure that you'll enjoy studying more about the Holy Spirit. The more you find out about Him, the more you'll be learning about your power source for growing as a Christian. Here are some books that we think you'll find helpful:

> A great book on the person and work of the Holy Spirit is entitled *The Divine Comforter*. It's by a guy with a great name for an author who writes about the Holy Spirit: J. Dwight Pentecost.
>
> *Basic Theology* by Charles C. Ryrie has ten chapters on the Holy Spirit. (Don't worry; they're short chapters.)
>
> We like the section on the Holy Spirit in Dr. James Boice's classic book *Foundations of the Christian Faith*.
>
> *Operating in the Power of the Holy Spirit* by Larry Keefauver isn't really a book. It's set up as a 30-day devotional guide. You can go through it by yourself or in a group.
>
> Ronald E. Baxter does an excellent job of defining and classifying the spiritual gifts in his book *Gifts of the Spirit*.

# $\mathcal{Q}$uestions for $\mathcal{R}$eflection and $\mathcal{D}$iscussion

1. Read what Jesus said at the Last Supper to the disciples about the Holy Spirit in John 14:15-18,23-26. Do you think the disciples had any idea of what Jesus was talking about? What might have been their misconceptions? Did you have any misconceptions about the Holy Spirit before you read this chapter?

2. Are you excited or a bit apprehensive about the prospects of the Holy Spirit working in you in a supernatural way? Why?

3. Explain what it means for the Holy Spirit to "indwell" every Christian. How does this "indwelling" differ from the "filling" of the Holy Spirit?

4. Name some of the ways in which the Holy Spirit helps a believer grow as a Christian.

5. What is the difference between fruit of the Spirit and spiritual gifts?

6. Do you have a sense of what spiritual gift you may possess? Can you identify a spiritual gift in other Christians you know?

◻ ◻ ◻

## Moving On...

The power of the Holy Spirit will be wasted unless you allow Him to put it to use in your life. For example,

- You can't expect the Holy Spirit to guide you in understanding God's Word unless you actually read the Bible.

- Nor can He help you talk to God unless you are praying.

- He's available to guide you in sharing your faith with others, but you'll have to get things started.

- And you won't see much of a spiritual gift in action if you aren't involved in fellowship with other Christians in a church.

Beginning with the next chapter, we'll discuss some of these basic activities that should be a part of your Christian life. And we can't think of a better way to kick it off than with reading the Bible.

# Chapter 3

> The Bible was written so that anyone who wants to know who God is and how they are to live in a way that pleases Him can read it and find out.
>
> *Kay Arthur*

As a Christian, you know that Jesus has saved you and that the Holy Spirit has given you the power you need to live for Christ. You would think that would be enough to help you grow as a Christian, but God has given you even more—His very Word, the Bible. You can do many things that will help you grow as a Christian, but none is more important than getting into the habit of reading and studying the Bible.

Unfortunately, many Christians take a haphazard approach to their Bible reading and Bible study, as if they really didn't matter. What a mistake! What they don't understand is that the Bible is God's primary way of communicating with us. He gave us His Word so that we could get to know Him better and discover how He wants us to live.

Do you want to please God in all you do? Do you want to live a satisfied and meaningful life? Do you want to grow as a Christian? Then you need to immerse yourself in God's Word.

# The Bible:
# Read It for Life

*T*here is nothing boring about God, and there is nothing boring about the Bible. As we are about to explain, God has worked miracles to bring His Word into a format that is available and understandable to you. He wouldn't have done that just so your Bible could sit on the shelf. He wants you to read it because He has much that He wants to tell you. When you realize that the Bible is God's personal message to you, you'll be anxious to read all that the Bible has to say.

## There's No Other Book like It

You won't find anything to read more interesting or more valuable than the Bible. No other book ever written is like it. The

Bible uses almost every literary style: poetry, musical lyrics, historical narration, instruction, biographies, and even a few dream sequences. In terms of content, it's got everything you could be looking for:

- *High drama.* The Bible is the story of humankind's rebellion against God and of God's plan to restore a relationship with humanity. It includes an interesting subplot of Satan's failed mutiny and his continued attempts to thwart the human race's reconciliation with God. The stories, plots, and characters are timeless and present the full range of human emotions.

- *Great adventure.* The Bible contains political intrigue, travel on the high seas, and episodes in which men are pitted against the elements of nature. Those "survivor" TV shows have nothing on the Bible.

- *Incredible action.* You'll find true-life stories of wars and battles within the pages of the Bible. Whether reporting man-to-man combat or gigantic massacres, the Bible tells these stories in graphic detail.

- *Tender romance.* As the inventor of love (and sex), God knows how to write a good love story. The Bible includes stories of romantic relationships and love poetry.

- *Lofty philosophy.* The wit, wisdom, and philosophical ruminations of the world's wisest people are contained within the Bible.

- *Intricate science.* Although it is not a textbook, the Bible touches on the sciences of astronomy, geology, biology, and physiology, to name just a few.

- *Comprehensive history.* The Bible covers the spectrum of history, reaching back to a time before the universe began. You can't get much more historical than that. The progress of humankind from Adam to the first century A.D. is covered in detail.

- *Apocalyptic prophesies.* The Bible doesn't stop with just a past historical perspective. It projects forward with prophecies about how the world will end.

Most importantly, the Bible stands out as a holy book. More than any other religious text, the Bible is read by people looking for spiritual answers to their deepest questions.

## The Bible Is God's Personal Message to You

If you are having difficulty getting motivated to read the Bible, change the way you view it. Don't think of it as a ponderous religious book. Instead, realize that the Bible is God's personal message to you. He has something important to say to you. He knows you better than anyone else, and He knows exactly what you need to hear. If God sent you an e-mail or a letter, you would open and read it right away. Well, think of the Bible the same way. It's God's personal letter He wants you to read.

### You've Got to Read It for Yourself

Maybe you are fully convinced that the Bible is the most valuable resource in the world, but you don't have any available slots in your daily planner for the time-intensive luxury of reading. Maybe you are wondering if you can realize the same benefits by using your morning commute time to listen to audiotapes of the Bible (read by some actor like James Earl Jones so it sounds like the voice of God). Or maybe you are tempted to pop a dramatized version of the Bible into your video player while exercising on your treadmill ("Sweating with the Psalms"—it's got infomercial potential).

You'll get a benefit whenever and however you bring the Bible into your thought processes. But you'll get the best benefit when you get it straight from the Bible and without distractions.

Reading the Bible works best because it demands your focused attention. Besides, Bible reading is intimate—it's just you and God. God can speak to you in the quietness of your Bible study time.

> *Be silent, and know that I am God!* (Psalm 46:10).

And the Holy Spirit can help you understand what you are reading.

> *No one can know God's thoughts except God's own Spirit. And God has actually given us his Spirit (not the world's spirit) so we can know the wonderful things God has freely given us* (1 Corinthians 2:11-12).

---

## *I*s There a Difference Between Reading and Studying the Bible?

Definitely, yes! Reading is good, but studying is better. Reading doesn't necessarily involve a method. You can read without paying attention to what is written (as any college student reading a textbook at the beach can attest). Reading is often what makes the Bible so frustrating for people. The apparent futility is not from lack of desire or time or motivation. People often lose interest because they merely *read* the Bible rather than implementing a method for *studying* the Bible. Although we may use the terms *reading* and *studying* interchangeably, we're almost always referring to studying: the deliberate and disciplined attempt to read, understand, and apply what the Bible says. We will get into specifics about different types of study methods in the next chapter. For now, we'll just say that studying requires that you do two things:

- *Intake:* Make an effort to really learn what the Bible says (2 Timothy 2:15).

- *Meditate:* Think deeply about God's Word and how it impacts your life (Psalm 1:2).

---

## God Said It, and You Can Believe It

Here's another reason to study the Bible: The Bible is the only thing you will ever read that is guaranteed to be 100 percent true. You can't say that about any other book. When you read the Bible, you know that you are getting God's divine discourse and not some human opinion. God can't lie (see 1 Samuel 15:29; Titus 1:2; and Hebrews 6:18), so what He says in the Bible must be true. God presents things as they really are whether He is talking about Himself or some aspect of His creation.

But you don't have to take our word for it. Jesus Christ spoke of the Word of God as being the truth in this prayer to His heavenly Father:

> *Make them pure and holy by teaching them your words of truth* (John 17:17).

---

# *D*oesn't the Bible Have Some Inconsistencies?

If the God of truth wrote the Bible, then it must be inerrant (without any errors). The credibility of the Bible rests upon the principle of inerrancy. If it is false in even only a few respects, then it is not wholly truthful. And if the Bible is wrong about the minor things, then maybe it's wrong about the major ones. Where does that leave you? How can you determine what is wrong and what is right? Fortunately, you don't need to lose sleep over this issue. For centuries people have been trying to disprove the Bible, but no one has been successful.

You are correct if you think that the Bible contains some *apparent* inconsistencies. For example, the Gospels give different stories about the women who went to the tomb of Jesus and found it empty. Mark 16:5 reports that "they entered the tomb, and there on the right sat a young man clothed in a white robe." But Luke 24:4 says that "suddenly, two men appeared to them, clothed in dazzling robes." So what was it? Two or one? Is this an inconsistency that proves that the Bible is unreliable?

Dr. Charles Ryrie explains that inerrancy means that the Bible tells the truth, but truth can include approximations, free quotations, and different accounts of the same event as long as these do not contradict. For example, the reference in 1 Corinthians 10:8 that says 23,000 died in one day doesn't contradict the report in Numbers 25:9 that 24,000 died at the same event (because the Numbers verse doesn't add the restriction of "in one day").

Other apparent inconsistencies can be explained as approximations. For example, you might tell a friend that you took three hours to drive home in a storm. And you might even add a phrase like, "and that is the absolute truth." Your approximation would be the truth even if you really drove for three hours and seven minutes. Don't use any false claim of inconsistencies as an excuse. You can trust the Bible to be inerrant. For that reason alone it deserves to be read.

## How the Bible Got from God to You

The Bible is not just thoughts about God written by a bunch of guys in beards and sandals. The Bible represents the very Word of God Himself (that's why the Bible is called "the Word of God"). But God used a bunch of guys—most of whom were in beards and sandals—to write down His words.

> *Long ago God spoke many times and in many ways to our ancestors through the prophets* (Hebrews 1:1).

So how did the Bible get here in the first place? How did God's Word get from His thoughts to your Bible? In his book *A General Introduction to the Bible*, Dr. Norman Geisler explains that God's Word passed through three "links" in the chain from God to you: *inspiration, canonization,* and *transmission.* Let's take a look at each of these.

### The Bible from God to You: Inspiration

The first link in the chain is called *inspiration.* In the literal sense of the word, *inspire* means "to breathe or blow into," and that's what God did. Using the Holy Spirit, God literally breathed His words into 40 different human writers (most of whom were called "prophets") over a 1600-year time period to write down His message for humankind. Here's how the Bible describes it:

> *Above all, you must understand that no prophecy in Scripture ever came from the prophets themselves or because they wanted to prophesy. It was the Holy Spirit who moved the prophets to speak from God* (2 Peter 1:20-21).

Even Webster's dictionary acknowledges the uniqueness of inspiration, defining it as "a divine influence." Because of this process, you can trust the Bible completely, even if you don't understand everything about the Bible. God, who is perfect, used a foolproof means to get His message into print. God "breathed in" what He wanted. Nothing more, nothing less. And all of it is inspired and valuable.

# God Isn't a Dictator

When God inspired the human authors to write down His message, He didn't speak into some kind of divine Dictaphone. Instead, the Holy Spirit communicated the message of God through each human writer, who then wrote down the words using his own style and personality. That's why different books of the Bible have different writing styles.

### The Bible from God to You: Canonization

The second link in the chain is *canonicity*, which is the process by which church leaders recognized individual books of the Bible as being inspired by God. The *canon* describes the collection of books that make up the Bible we use today. The word comes from the root word *reed*. Reeds were used as measuring sticks in ancient times.

When applied to the Bible, *canon* indicates the measure or the standard used to evaluate which books were inspired and which ones weren't. The final book of the Bible to be inspired by God was the book of Revelation. The apostle John, who was the human author, finished writing Revelation at the end of the first century. For the next few hundred years, several church councils met to determine which books should be included in the canon of Scripture. Their main task was to evaluate books written during and after the time of Christ (the Old Testament canon had already been determined). According to Dr. Geisler, the councils followed strict guidelines in order to determine whether or not a book was inspired by God. They asked themselves,

1. Does it speak with God's authority?

2. Is it written by a man of God speaking to us as a prophet of God?

3. Does it have the authentic stamp of God?

4. Does it impact us with the power of God?

5. Was it accepted by the people of God?

It is important to know that the canon councils did not *declare* a book to be from God. They simply *recognized* the divine influence that was already there.

### The Bible from God to You: Transmission

The third link in the chain has nothing to do with your car. *Transmission* describes the total process of transmitting the Bible from the early writers to us today using the most practical and reliable methods and materials available. According to Geisler, "The Scriptures had to be copied, translated, recopied, and retranslated. This process not only provided the Scriptures for other nations, but for other generations as well."

---

## *I*nfallibility and Inerrancy

When we say the Bible is infallible or inerrant, we mean that it is completely true. This is because God, who is the author, is incapable of error. However, this doesn't mean that today's Bible translations are completely without error. Only the original manuscripts were absolutely correct.

---

The whole Bible didn't come at one time. As we said before, God inspired 40 different authors over a period of 1600 years to write the Bible. With all of the materials and people involved, how did God make sure that His Word was transmitted accurately from one person to the next, from one generation to the next, and from one century to the next? Since Xerox machines and printing presses didn't exist back then, God's people needed a reliable way to copy the Scriptures so His Word could be accurately transmitted and preserved.

Beginning hundreds of years before Christ, Jewish scribes (you could call them professional human copiers) had to follow detailed procedures and rules for copying Scripture. These rules helped ensure complete concentration and accuracy. Their meticulous approach set the standard for monks and other scholars who transcribed the Bible through the ages. Here are just three rules for scribes (Jewish scholar Samuel Davidson lists dozens) that will give you some idea as to the painstaking detail involved in copying God's Word:

1. No word or letter or any other mark may be written from memory. The scribe must look directly at the original scroll for every stroke.

2. Between every letter, the space of a hair or thread must intervene.

3. Should a king address a scribe while the scribe is writing the name of God, the scribe must take no notice of the king until finished.

---

# *T*he Reliability and Accuracy of God's Word

Scholars have a way of determining if ancient documents are reliable and accurate. First, how many copies exist of a document? The more copies there are, the more chance you have to compare the copies and test the accuracy. Archaeologists have uncovered more copies of ancient Bible manuscripts than of any other document of antiquity. More than 5000 various manuscripts of the New Testament Scriptures alone are available today!

Second, how close to the date of the first manuscript are the copies? The Bible shines in this area as well. In 1947 some Bedouins found ancient scrolls in a cave in Jordan. Scholars drooled over this magnificent discovery (although they were careful not to drool on the scrolls), which they called the Dead Sea scrolls. Before the discovery of these scrolls, the oldest complete copy of the Old Testament was dated 1400 years after the Old Testament was completed. The Dead Sea scrolls closed the gap by a thousand years, and they showed that the Bible text had been transmitted accurately.

The third test of reliability and accuracy has to do with the corroborating evidence. In other words, are there any other historical documents that confirm the claims of the Bible? The answer is a resounding yes. Not every person, date, or fact in the Bible has been verified by outside sources, but many have, and not one has been shown to be false. The evidence for the accuracy of the Bible from sources outside the Bible is nothing short of miraculous.

---

### The Language of God's Word

The materials used to write down God's Word were important, and so were the detailed methods of transcribing the words. But what about the means of communication? What about the words themselves, which are at the heart of God's Word? Once again, God was involved in this process, which we call *language*.

The two original languages of the Bible are Hebrew (Old Testament) and Greek (New Testament). God didn't choose these languages at random, but rather for specific purposes, including accuracy, reliability, and understanding. The languages God chose were the best possible for communicating His message to us.

- *Hebrew*—Language experts agree that Hebrew, the principle language of the Old Testament and of the Jewish (or Hebrew) people is precise, pictorial, and personal. Hebrew has been called the perfect biographical language because it describes a God who is very much involved in the lives of people, especially His chosen people, the Jews.

- *Greek*—One of the reasons God chose Greek as the language of the New Testament is that this was the language spoken by most of the world at the time Jesus Christ lived on the earth. Greek has been called the perfect intellectual language, which was ideal for expressing the propositional truth of the New Testament.

### Translating the Original Languages

*Translating* simply means changing from one language to another while retaining the meaning of the original language. The first translation of the Old Testament came in the third or second century B.C., when the Hebrew Scriptures were translated into Greek so more people could read them. It was called the Septuagint (from the Latin word for 70) because 70 scholars worked on the translation. The entire Bible was translated into Latin in A.D. 405 (it was called the Vulgate), and that remained the authoritative Bible translation for the next thousand years.

The first English version of the Bible didn't come until 1384, when John Wycliffe translated the Bible from the Latin Vulgate.

In 1530 William Tyndale finished translating the Bible from the original languages into English. The Geneva Bible (also known as the Puritan Bible, because this is the Bible the Pilgrims brought to America on the Mayflower in 1620) was produced in 1560. The King James Version, the most popular English translation ever, was first published in 1611. Many of the "modern" English translations we read today were written in the twentieth century.

## The Bible and the Printing Press

As recently as the fifteenth century, scribes took ten months to copy the Bible by hand, and a single copy cost more money than the average person made in a lifetime. Besides that, few people knew how to read. Then came Johannes Gutenberg and his printing press, generally acknowledged to be the most significant invention of the last thousand years. The first book Gutenberg printed in 1455 was a Latin version of the Bible. Within 50 years, hundreds of Gutenberg presses were producing thousands of Bibles. The price of a Bible dropped dramatically, people learned how to read, and the world has not been the same since.

### The Bible Is All About Everything You Need to Know

If you're still looking for a reason to study the Bible, try this: It tells you everything that you need to know. Oh sure, it doesn't include a troubleshooting guide for when you can't seem to get connected to your new Internet service provider, and it won't tell you whether you need to carry an umbrella with you tomorrow. But it does tell you about the important things in life—things like God, human nature, and other eternal mysteries of the universe. In the long run, aren't you a little more worried about "life after death" than about reading your e-mail or getting wet?

### The Bible Is All About God

Have you ever wondered if God is real? Well, there is one way to find out. Start looking for Him. And there is no better place to start than in the Bible. You won't have to look too hard. God isn't hiding from you. This isn't a game of celestial hide-and-seek. God wants you to find Him, and He promises that you will if you are serious about your search:

> *"If you look for me in earnest, you will find me when you seek me. I will be found by you," says the* Lord *(Jeremiah 29:13-14).*

If you want to find God, read the Bible.

### The Bible Is All About Human Nature

Don't ever think that the Bible is just a bunch of boring, out-dated philosophical and historical ramblings. What you can read in the Bible has practical and relevant application to your life. How is that possible? Because God knows all about you. God knows your innermost thoughts, and He uses the Bible as His means to get through to you:

> *For the word of God is full of living power. It is sharper than the sharpest knife, cutting deep into our innermost thoughts and desires. It exposes us for what we really are* (Hebrews 4:12).

But that's not all. The Bible has supernatural power (because it was written by a supernatural Being) to overcome our natural failings and frailties. So when we are disoriented in life, the Bible can set us straight:

> *Your word is a lamp for my feet and a light for my path* (Psalm 119:105).

And the Bible can even give us supernatural strength to resist temptation:

> *I have hidden your word in my heart, that I might not sin against you* (Psalm 119:11).

That's the kind of stuff you'll discover in the Bible. Is that relevant and personal enough for you?

### The Bible Is All About the Secrets of the Universe

Yes, the big secrets of the universe are explained in the Bible, such as how the world began and how it is going to end. That ought to tweak your interest a little bit. If knowing where you came from, where you are going, or how you are going to end up is of interest to you, it's all in the Bible. The most important secret revealed in the Bible is how sinful people can be made right with a holy God. Not only does the Bible explain God's plan of salvation and how you can obtain it, but the Bible also gives detailed instructions for how you can get to know God intimately. Think of it! You and God are able to share thoughts with one another. Of course, that won't happen by itself. You'll have to read the Bible to learn how you can grow close in your relationship with God.

## Read the Bible for Life

Are you sick and tired of your "same old, same old" routine? Do you feel as if you are going nowhere? Are you anxious for your life to be significant? Then the Bible is the book you've got to read. Look at what the Bible says that it can do for you:

> All Scripture is inspired by God and is useful to teach us what is true and to make us realize what is wrong in our lives. It straightens us out and teaches us to do what is right. It is God's way of preparing us in every way, fully equipped for every good thing God wants us to do (2 Timothy 3:16-17).

These verses give every reason you need to get serious about studying the Bible if you are serious about having a life that means anything. Look at what these verses promise:

- *Motivation:* "All Scripture is inspired by God...." Forget reading books by motivational gurus. If you really want to get growing in your life, go to the book that is written by the world's best motivational mentor: God.

- *Instruction:* "…And is useful to teach us what is true…." There is a lot of bad advice out there. But you can trust what you read in the Bible to be true.

- *Detection:* "…And to make us realize what is wrong in our lives…." The Bible may be the therapist you need to help you discover what is going wrong in your life.

- *Correction*: "It straightens us out…." After you find out what is wrong in your life, you are going to have to make a few changes. The Bible can tell you exactly how to fix the broken parts of your life.

- *Direction:* "…and teaches us to do what is right." We can't rely on our own instincts to decide what is right and wrong. (Our own instincts got us into trouble in the first place.) The Bible can give us a new and improved value system.

- *Preparation:* "It is God's way of preparing us in every way…." While other people, books, and sermons may be of some value, the best help you'll get is from God, and His instruction manual is the Bible.

- *Realization*: "…fully equipped for every good thing God wants us to do." God's Word doesn't get outdated, and it is not incomplete. It contains everything you need to know to become—and to do—all that God has planned for you.

As 2 Timothy 3:16-17 makes clear, the Bible can give you everything you need to improve your life. Of course, that only happens if you start studying the Bible. (A Bible stuck on the bookshelf won't change you by osmosis.) But you don't have to wait six to eight weeks for the Bible to start delivering on its promises. The benefits that come from studying the Bible will begin as soon as you start reading.

- You will be pleasing God (2 Timothy 2:15).

- You will immediately begin to grow and mature spiritually because you'll be getting the spiritual nourishment that you need (1 Peter 2:2).

- You will develop spiritual discernment to know whether other people are speaking the truth about God (Acts 17:11).

- You will be able to answer the questions that other people have about God, and you will be able to give clear answers to those who ask you about your faith (1 Peter 3:15).

Why should you study the Bible? Because that is the way you are going to get the life that God has intended for you all along. What are you waiting for?

## What's That Again?

1. The Bible contains almost every literary style and all the drama, adventure, romance, history, and prophecy you could ever want.

2. You will benefit the most from what the Bible has to say if you read and study it for yourself.

3. The Bible is the only book you will ever read with a 100 percent truth guarantee. That's because God, who is incapable of lying, is the author.

4. There are three "links" in the chain from God to your Bible: inspiration, canonization, and transmission.

5. The original languages of the Bible were Hebrew and Greek. A Bible translation is a version that has been translated from the original languages into another language.

6. The Bible tells us about the important things in life, such as God, human nature, and the mysteries of the universe.

7. Reading and studying the Bible will result in an improved life, and it will please God.

## Dig Deeper

Here are some basic books to help you better understand the Bible:

> *How to Read the Bible for All Its Worth* by Gordon Fee and Douglas Stuart is an easy-to-read book with a good section on choosing a Bible translation.

> *What the Bible Is All About* by Henrietta Mears is the best selling book about the Bible ever written. The reason is that it's personal and readable.

> Our book, *Knowing the Bible 101,* is a companion book to this one. It includes an overview of every section and every book in the Bible.

> If you want to know more about the reliability of the Bible, we suggest the first section of *A Ready Defense* by Josh McDowell.

> If those apparent inconsistencies are troubling you, then you might like to read *735 Baffling Bible Questions Answered* by Larry Richards. If you've got questions about the Bible, Dr. Richards has the answers.

# *Q*uestions for *R*eflection and *D*iscussion

1. List three reasons why you should read the Bible. Which one of these is the most compelling to you?

2. Read John 16:12-13 and 1 Corinthians 2:10-12. How does the Holy Spirit help you understand the Bible? Now read 1 Corinthians 2:14. Is this same understanding available to the non-Christian? Why or why not?

3. What does it mean to study the Bible? How is this different from merely reading the Bible? What is involved in Bible meditation and what are the benefits (see Joshua 1:8)?

4. Has any *apparent* inconsistency in the Bible been especially troubling to you? What have you done to resolve this issue? What more could you do?

5. What is the significance of the fact that the canon councils did not *declare* the Bible to be God's Word, but simply *recognized* the divine influence that was already there? Make a comparison between this process and a scientist making a discovery (such as Newton discovering the law of gravity).

6. How does the evidence for the Bible's reliability from history and archaeology give you confidence as you read it? What if the Bible were not a reliable document? How would that affect the Bible's main message?

7. Give an example of something the Bible says about human nature. How does this compare to something a popular book might say about human nature?

## Moving On...

By now you've gotten the idea that the key to using your Bible is to read and study it. But just exactly *how* do you study the Bible? Do you start in Genesis and read all the way through to Revelation, or do you pick and choose what you want to read? How often should you read the Bible, and for how long? And what about all of those books—66 in all? How do you make sense of everything?

In the next chapter we're going to give you an overview of how the Bible is organized, and we're going to suggest several different approaches to reading the Bible. You're not going to get this stuff overnight. It's going to take time. But it will be time well spent because the more you learn about the Bible, the better it gets.

# Chapter 4

One of the greatest tragedies today is that, although the Bible is an available, open book, it is a closed book to millions— either because they leave it unread or because they read it without applying its teachings to themselves.

*Henrietta Mears*

We'll admit it so you don't have to: The Bible can be difficult to read. But it doesn't have to be. The main source of frustration is usually a matter of disorientation. In the time that it takes to turn a page, the context of the Bible can quickly change from history to poetry, from B.C. to A.D., or from a biography to a letter. If you get lost on a road trip, you can't enjoy the scenery around you because you are too worried about finding out where you are. But once you get your bearings and find a map, you can enjoy the journey. It's all a matter of orientation.

It's the same way with the Bible. You can enjoy and get more out of your study when you know the context. That's what this chapter is all about. We're going to give you a map for the Bible. Enjoy the trip.

# How to Really Study the Bible

*P*eople who never study the Bible have a lot of misconceptions about the Bible, including these: It's difficult to study, it's full of myths and contradictions, and it has no relevance to daily life. People who study the Bible find just the opposite to be true. They know that the Bible is clear, correct, and practical. If you haven't found that to be the case, don't worry. Nothing is wrong with you, and nothing is wrong with the Bible. You simply haven't studied enough to make sense of what you have read. In this chapter we want to suggest that you approach your study of God's Word by learning how to properly interpret the Bible. But first you have to get the big picture.

## The Big Picture

Even though the Bible is a collection of 66 separate books, it follows a chronological order—sort of. More impressive than that, it tells one basic story: *the relationship between God and people.* Once you understand that basic plot and where you are in the story line, everything you read will make sense. Here is how the story of that great drama of the relationship of God and humanity is laid out:

## 1. Perfect Fellowship

The first two chapters of the Bible describe how God created Adam and Eve, and how the three of them had a great friendship going. Everything was perfect in the Garden of Eden. This part of the God/human drama takes only about 56 verses to tell because, unfortunately, it didn't last very long.

## 2. The Relationship Was Broken

People sinned, and the rest of the Old Testament and the first four books of the New Testament describe the details of God's plan to restore the relationship.

*The consequence of Adam's sin.* Adam and Eve exercised their own free will and chose to follow their desires instead of God's instructions. Their disobedience plunged the entire human race into misery and separation from God. The intimate relationship with God was broken because of humanity's sin.

*The judgments that accompany sin.* Sin always results in separation from God and brings consequences. Humanity's continual rebellion against God—and the consequences—are illustrated by the Bible's historical reports of episodes such as Adam and Eve's expulsion from the Garden of Eden, the Great Flood (in which only Noah and his family were spared), and God's confusing everyone's language at the Tower of Babel.

*God's chosen people.* God wanted to show the world that people who follow His laws receive His blessings. He selected the descendants of Abraham (later called Jews or Israelites) to be His chosen people for this purpose. God also planned to bring Jesus into the world through Abraham's bloodline. Genesis introduces the story of Abraham in chapter 12 and ends with his descendants living in Egypt.

*God lays down the law.* By Exodus 20, Moses had led the Israelites out of slavery in Egypt. God gave to Moses the Ten Commandments, which showed the standard of behavior that God finds acceptable. As is illustrated throughout the Old Testament, no one is able to keep all of the commandments. No one is able to live up to God's perfect standard. The Israelites were perfect examples of imperfect people, and as a result of their disobedience to God's command to enter the promised land, God sent them to wander in the desert for 40 years.

*A nation finds a place to call home.* When the Israelites' time of judgment was completed, God led them into the promised land, and their nation was established. But life was a constant battle (literally) because they continued to disobey God's explicit directives. The people rejected the theocracy (God's supervision through judges) and demanded a king. God gave them what they wanted even though He knew it was not best for them.

Over the centuries, Israel prospered under kings who listened to God, and it suffered under kings who ignored Him. Israel was continually at war with the neighboring nations. The people seemed to forget that their nation prospered when it followed God and suffered when it ignored Him. The nation of Israel started to deteriorate as it was invaded by its adversaries. The country was decimated when most of its population was taken captive and held in exile. Little by little, the Jews were able to return to their homeland and rebuild the city of Jerusalem.

*The cry of the prophets.* God used prophets as His messengers to warn the people of the consequences of their disobedience and to implore them to turn back to God. The prophets had mixed results. Usually they were ignored, which may account for why they seemed so irritable. Some of these prophets lived while Israel was in its homeland; others spoke during the times of exile.

*The promised Messiah arrives.* A 400-year gap separates the Old Testament and the New Testament. The Jews were back in their homeland, waiting for the Messiah. God had promised to Abraham that reconciliation with God would come through his descendants, and He had promised the Jews that the Messiah would establish a new kingdom on earth. The first four books of the New Testament (the Gospels) are the biography of Jesus, the promised Messiah.

## 3. The Relationship Can Be Restored

God's relationship with humanity could only be restored by solving the sin problem. Only someone who was perfect could pay the penalty for our sin. (That eliminated all of humankind because no one but Jesus could pass the Ten Commandments test.) The death of Jesus Christ on the cross was the sacrifice that God had planned all along.

*The penalty paid.* The death of Jesus paid the penalty for humanity's sin. It is the focal point of the entire Bible because it is the seminal event for reconciling humankind to God. The story of the death and resurrection of Christ is told in each of the four Gospels.

*Maturing is a process.* The followers of Christ during the first century were a ragtag group, but their numbers grew rapidly as the Christian message spread through the Middle East and parts of Europe. Small churches were established by missionaries such as the apostle Paul. Some of the disciples wrote letters to these churches to explain concepts about accepting Christ as Savior and then growing in a deeper relationship with Him.

*Reunited at the end.* The Bible ends appropriately with a look into the future. The book of Revelation describes the events that will mark the end of the world (as we know it), including the second coming of Jesus Christ and the establishment of God's eternal kingdom, where Christians will live with Him forever.

And there you have it: a basic outline for the greatest drama the world will ever know. As you study the Bible, figure out where the passage that you are reading fits into the story line.

# An Interesting Subplot

*Star Wars* has nothing on the real-life intergalactic battle between the forces of God and evil. Before Adam and Eve, Satan was one of the highest-ranking angels. He attempted a mutiny against God, and it failed. Ever since, Satan has been trying to thwart God's plan. Throughout the Bible you can see Satan's attempts to interfere in humankind's reconciliation to God.

## Know Where You Are Before You Get Going

Now that you know the big picture of the Bible, let's break it down a bit. We'll list the books of the Bible according to their traditional categories. Before you study any portion of the Bible, you should recognize what category you are in. Once you know the category, you'll have a basic orientation for what you are about to read.

The Bible is divided into two parts: the Old Testament and the New Testament. The names are a bit misleading because they are both really old. But think of it this way: The Old Testament takes place before Jesus was born, and the New Testament starts with the birth of Christ. (That isn't exactly correct because some parts of the Old Testament refer to future stuff that hasn't even happened yet, but most people won't be that nitpicky.)

### The Old Testament Books

Think of the Old Testament as a historical record of God's chosen people, the Jews. It covers the time from before Creation up to about 432 B.C. The Old Testament contains 39 books, and they are traditionally divided into these four categories:

### 1. The Books of Moses—How It All Began

Moses wrote the first five books of the Bible. They tell how things started, including the beginning of the world, the beginning of mankind, the beginning of sin, the beginning of judgment, and the beginning of the Jews.

- Genesis

- Exodus

- Leviticus

- Numbers

- Deuteronomy

## 2. The Books of Generals, Judges, and Kings—War and Peace

If the first five books of the Bible are about the birth and early years of the human race, then the next 12 books are about the adolescence of the human race. And if you say that word slow enough, it sounds like "add less sense." That describes the Israelites because they acted like a bunch of teenagers rebelling against their heavenly Father. These books tell the up-and-down history of Israel as a nation.

- Joshua

- Judges

- Ruth

- 1 and 2 Samuel

- 1 and 2 Kings

- 1 and 2 Chronicles

- Ezra

- Nehemiah

- Esther

## 3. The Books of Poetry and Wisdom—a Way with Words

Up to this point, the books of the Bible have pretty much been in chronological order (with a little overlap). But the books in this category stop the chronological flow. This group includes a collection of lyrical books of poetry and prose about the character of God.

- Job
- Psalms
- Proverbs
- Ecclesiastes
- Song of Songs

## 4. The Books of the Prophets—Grumpy Old Men

Like the poetry books, this category doesn't add to the Bible's time line. The books of the prophets were written before, during, and after the Jews were taken captive and lived in exile in Assyria, Babylonia, and Persia (category 2 above). Don't think that these books are outdated manifestos written by a bunch of lunatics. The prophets knew what they were talking about. For example, every one of their predictions about the birth and death of Jesus came true. When you see that kind of accuracy, you ought to pay close attention to what they wrote about God and their predictions for the end of the world. This category is often divided into two subgroups: the Major Prophets and the Minor Prophets. The distinction has nothing to do with ability (like the major and minor leagues in baseball). It simply refers to the length of the books.

### *Major Prophets*

- Isaiah
- Ezekiel
- Jeremiah
- Daniel
- Lamentations

### *Minor Prophets*

- Hosea
- Nahum
- Joel
- Habakkuk
- Amos
- Zephaniah
- Obadiah
- Haggai
- Jonah
- Zechariah
- Micah
- Malachi

## The New Testament Books

Think of the New Testament as a historical record of the birth and life of Jesus and the ministry of His followers, whose faith grew after His death and resurrection. Nine different authors wrote the 27 books of the New Testament, and the writings cover a time span of less than 100 years (not counting the prophecy of future events contained in Revelation). The New Testament books are traditionally divided up into these four categories:

## 1. The Gospels—the Life of Christ in Surround Sound

The first four books of the New Testament are all biographies, and they are all about the same person: Jesus. Why do we need *four* different biographies of the same person? Because each of them is written by a different author who takes a different perspective. These books are named after their authors.

- Matthew        - Luke

- Mark           - John

## 2. The Book of Acts—the Church Is Born

This category contains only one book, but it includes the incredible story of those first Christians in the years immediately following the resurrection of Christ. These were people who were accused of turning "the rest of the world upside down" (Acts 17:6).

## 3. The Epistles—the Bible Mailbag

These 21 books aren't really books at all. They are letters. They were written to churches or to individuals and contained instructions about how to live the Christian life. Our lifestyle today may be a lot different from the lives of people who lived 2000 years ago, but the fears and problems those early Christians struggled with are pretty much the same as ours.

- Romans
- 1 and 2 Corinthians
- Galatians
- Ephesians
- Philippians
- Colossians
- 1 and 2 Thessalonians
- 1 and 2 Timothy
- Titus
- Philemon
- Hebrews
- James
- 1 and 2 Peter
- 1, 2, and 3 John
- Jude

### 4. The Book of Revelation—How It's Going to End

The final category has only one book, but it's a good thing. The world couldn't handle more than one book like this. No book of the Bible has been more analyzed, pondered, or puzzled over. It's fitting that this book is the last one of the Bible because it proclaims the end of time for the world and the beginning of the rest of eternity.

## How to Interpret the Bible

The most valuable thing you can do as you study the Bible is to bring out the meaning. This is also known as *interpretation*. When you interpret something, you make it plain and understandable. Gordon Fee and Douglas Stuart write that the interpreter (that's you) has two tasks:

1. The interpreter needs to be engaged in "careful, systematic study of the Scripture to discover the original, intended meaning" (this is called *exegesis*). You don't read the Bible only when you feel like it or only on Sundays. As an interpreter, you are in the Word daily.

2. The interpreter needs to seek "the contemporary relevance of ancient texts" (this is called *hermeneutics*). In other words, you learn to apply what the Scripture says without contradicting the original meaning.

### Seven Habits of Highly Effective Interpreters

There are no two ways about it. If you want to be a good Bible interpreter, you need to work at it. Many people think that if they just read the Bible casually, amazing insights will come into their heads, but it doesn't work that way. Yes, the Holy Spirit will guide you "into all truth" (John 14:17), but you can't remain a passive bystander. You need to engage the brain God gave you, and that means developing your interpretation skills.

Getting good at Bible interpretation is no different from getting good at business, sports, science, or music. If you want to be a success, you have to observe the rules and follow the principles. Above all, it takes practice, practice, practice. Fortunately, you don't have to come up with your own principles. They are already out there, thanks to skilled and godly Bible teachers like Kay Arthur, who gives seven basic principles to help you interpret the Bible accurately.

*Principle 1: Remember that context rules.* Whenever you read a chapter, a verse, or even a word of Scripture, it must always be taken in context, which means "that which goes with the text." Context helps give meaning to the text you are studying. According to Kay Arthur, here's what you should ask yourself when you read the Bible: "Is my interpretation of a particular section of Scripture consistent with the theme, purpose, and structure of the book in which it is found?"

*Principle 2: Always seek the full counsel of the Word of God.* The more you know the entire Bible, the better you can correctly interpret individual passages or verses. Don't develop an idea on just one or two isolated verses, and don't accept teaching from someone who does. Remember, context is king, and this includes the context of the "full counsel" of the Bible. Kay Arthur advises, "Saturate yourself in the Word of God; it is your safeguard against wrong doctrine."

# The Rules of Context

Gordon Fee and Douglas Stuart talk about two kinds of context: historical and literary. Each book of the Bible has a different historical context, which has to do with the time and culture of the author and his readers. You have to ask why and when the book was written. What was going on in the culture at the time, and who are the major historical figures involved? To get a general sense of the historical context, read the introductory notes to the book in your Bible (if you have a study Bible) or look up the information in a Bible handbook.

The literary context of the Bible refers to the words themselves. All words have meaning, but they take on different meanings in a sentence or paragraph. For example, if Stan said the word *lawyer,* you would probably have negative thoughts. But if he said, "Bruce is a lawyer," then you would think happy thoughts. The word takes on a different meaning in context.

*Principle 3: Remember that Scripture will never contradict Scripture.* The Bible never contradicts itself because God cannot lie and cannot contradict Himself. If two passages of Scripture seem to be in contradiction, one of two things is going on. Either your interpretation of at least one of the two passages is wrong, or your understanding is limited. Sometimes our human minds are unable to grasp the truths and mysteries of an infinite God. Here's what God says:

> *"My thoughts are completely different from yours," says the* LORD. *"And my ways are far beyond anything you could imagine"* (Isaiah 55:8).

*D*on't think of doctrine as stuffy and boring. Doctrine forms the basis for what you believe. When it comes to the Bible and your faith, it's critical to have the correct doctrine, because that is what you ultimately believe to be true and correct.

*Principle 4: Do not base your doctrine on an obscure passage of Scripture.* Some verses and passages of Scripture are very difficult to understand. Don't build your faith on these. "Your doctrine should be based on the clear repeated teachings in the Scripture," says Kay Arthur. This doesn't mean you should abandon the more difficult verses. "What is obscure in one part of Scripture may be made clear in another," writes R.C. Sproul.

*Principle 5: Interpret Scripture literally.* What this means is that you should interpret the Bible *as it is written.* The Bible is a miraculous book, but it is not a magical book. God used the rules of grammar to communicate His message, which means a noun is always a noun and a verb is always a verb. "To interpret the Bible literally is to interpret it as *literature,*" Sproul writes. This means you have to look at literary form or style, such as poetry, prophecy, and historical narrative (we do this with everything we read). Is the author using a metaphor (figurative language) or hyperbole (deliberate exaggeration used for effect) to make a point? For example, when Jesus said your faith could move a mountain (Matthew 17:20), He didn't mean that you could literally move Mount Everest. Jesus was using a literary expression to show us just how potent our faith really is.

*Principle 6: Look for the author's intended meaning of the passage.* Don't read something into a verse or passage that isn't there, and don't skip over something that is. "Always try to understand what the author had in mind when you interpret a portion of the Bible," says Kay Arthur. "Let the passage speak for itself."

*Principle 7: Check your conclusions by using reliable commentaries.* When you read a passage of Scripture, you should always start with your own observations. Kay Arthur suggests that you pray before you begin, identify the context, observe the obvious, deal with the text objectively, and read with a purpose. Get up close and personal with the Bible by studying it directly. However, regardless of how knowledgeable you are, a good commentary (or a good Bible teacher) can be a plumb line for your own understanding and interpretation.

## Your Secret Weapon

Being a Christian gives you several advantages. First of all, there's that whole eternal life thing. How wonderful and comforting to know that because you have put your trust in God through the Person and work of Jesus Christ, you won't die spiritually but will have eternal life (John 3:16). But as important as your eternal destiny is, that's not all there is. The Christian life is more than having a fire insurance policy for eternity. Jesus said that He came to give us life "in all its fullness" (John 10:10). This includes the life you live in the here and now, not just in the hereafter. The most effective way to enjoy life in all its fullness is through the power of the Holy Spirit (in fact, it's the *only* way to live). "So I advise you to live according to your new life in the Holy Spirit," writes the apostle Paul. "Then you won't be doing what your sinful nature craves" (Galatians 5:16).

### Living in the Power of the Holy Spirit

When you live in the Spirit's power, you will be led by the Holy Spirit (Romans 8:13-14) and you will follow the Spirit (Romans 8:4). You will also desire to study God's Word. This makes perfect sense, because the Holy Spirit is God's Spirit in person—in you! When you invite God into your life by faith in Jesus, the Holy Spirit automatically enters your life in order to help you live the Christian life. And one of the most important things the Holy Spirit does is help you understand God's personal message to you, the Bible. Jesus gave us this promise:

> *And I will ask the Father, and he will give you another Counselor, who will never leave you. He is the Holy Spirit, who leads into all truth* (John 14:16-17).

The Holy Spirit is your secret weapon—your inside source—helping you to understand the things of God as you study His Word.

### Others Just Don't Get It

Do you ever get frustrated when people turn their backs to the things of God? Do you ever wonder why Christians are often ridiculed in the media? It's perfectly natural. Here's the deal. A Christian sees life from a supernatural perspective, but unbelievers have only their natural perspectives to go by. They just don't get it because the truth about God doesn't make sense to them. On the other hand, we get it because we have the Holy Spirit in our lives (1 Corinthians 2:14-15).

What an amazing thing to know! What an awesome responsibility! You see, just because you have the Holy Spirit doesn't mean that you will automatically have access to spiritual truth. When you harbor known sin in your life, you bring sorrow to the Holy Spirit (Ephesians 4:30). He's still in your life (and your fire insurance policy is still intact), but He can't do His work because God cannot tolerate sin. So what's the remedy? As usual, the Bible has the answer:

> *If we say we have no sin, we are only fooling ourselves and refusing to accept the truth. But if we confess our sins to him, he is faithful and just to forgive us and to cleanse us from every wrong. If we claim we have not sinned, we are calling God a liar and showing that his word has no place in our hearts* (1 John 1:8-10).

Do you want God's Word in your heart? Confess your sins to God. Do you want to keep from sinning? Then keep God's Word in your heart. As the psalmist David wrote, "I have hidden your word in my heart, that I might not sin against you" (Psalm 119:11).

# Bible Mysteries and Twisted Scripture

Just because you study hard and pray for guidance doesn't mean you are going to get everything God has said in His Word. Just because the Holy Spirit helps you understand the Bible doesn't mean you will understand everything in the Bible. Many things about God are a mystery to us, and so are certain things about God's Word. If God's thoughts are higher than our thoughts (Isaiah 55:8-9), then it stands to reason that some things in God's Word are beyond our understanding. When studying a verse or passage of Scripture, try not to find a meaning that just isn't there.

Likewise, avoid "twisting" Scripture to fit some preconceived idea. If you are using a verse or passage in the Bible to verify something you are doing, and if what you are doing is contrary to another area of the Bible, you are twisting Scripture and you need to stop. Likewise, you need to be on the lookout for other people, organizations, or churches that engage in Scripture twisting, which basically means they are interpreting the Bible to suit their own false beliefs. Paul confronted some members of the Galatian church who were falling prey to twisted Scripture: "You are already following a different way that pretends to be the Good News but is not the Good News at all. You are being fooled by those who twist and change the truth concerning Christ (Galatians 1:6-7).

## Study the Bible for Life

With all this talk about study and effort, you could conclude that studying the Bible is like taking a course in school (only without the grade). But there's much more to it than that. At its best, Bible study is a life-changing process, but only if you apply what the Bible says to your life. Kay Arthur explains:

Application flows out of thorough observation and correct interpretation. Application begins with belief, which then results in doing. It takes place as you are confronted with the truth and respond to it in obedience, and the glorious end result is transformation. You're made more like your Lord and Savior, Jesus Christ.

The Bible is much more blunt. If you don't apply what you learn, you are only fooling yourself.

> *And remember, it is a message to obey, not just to listen to. If you don't obey, you are only fooling yourself. For if you just listen and don't obey, it is like looking at your face in a mirror but doing nothing to improve your appearance. You see yourself, walk away, and forget what you look like. But if you keep looking steadily into God's perfect law—the law that sets you free—and if you do what it says and don't forget what you heard, then God will bless you for doing it* (James 1:22-25).

Do you want God to bless you? Do you want to live a life filled with God's transforming power? Then study the Bible, learn to interpret it correctly, and apply what it says to your life. There's no better way to live.

## What's That Again?

1. The Bible tells one basic story. It's about the relationship between God and people.

2. The story of that relationship can be summarized like this. At first there was perfect fellowship between God and humanity. Then the fellowship was broken, but it can be restored because of the death and resurrection of Jesus Christ, who will return once again before God establishes His eternal kingdom.

3. The Old Testament is the historical record of God's chosen people, the Jews. It covers the time from before creation up to 432 B.C.

4. The New Testament includes the historical record of the life of Jesus and the birth of the church, instructions about how to live as a Christian, and a description of the end of the world and the beginning of eternity.

5. The most valuable thing you can do as you study the Bible is to learn how to correctly interpret it, or bring out the meaning.

6. You will be mostly likely to get good at proper biblical interpretation if you follow certain principles. Among them are the principles about context, interpreting Scripture according to Scripture, interpreting the Bible as it is written, and looking for the author's intended meaning.

7. The Holy Spirit is your secret weapon as a Christian to help you understand the things of God and to study His Word.

8. Avoid changing or twisting the meaning of Scripture to fit some preconceived idea. Instead, learn how to interpret the Bible correctly and then apply what it says to your life.

## Dig Deeper

We can recommend several great books to help you get an overview of the Bible:

Our first suggestion is *Talk Thru the Bible* by Bruce Wilkinson and Kenneth Boa. If you like charts, tables, and outlines, you'll love this book.

If you want a narrative overview and summary of every book in the Bible, then you must read *Adventuring Through the Bible* by Ray C. Stedman.

*How to Study Your Bible* by Kay Arthur is extremely practical and easy to follow. Kay is a master teacher of the inductive Bible study approach, which builds on observation, interpretation, and application.

R.C. Sproul's *Knowing Scripture* lays the groundwork for Bible study by discussing why we should study the Bible and how our own personal study impacts interpretation.

---

◻ ◻ ◻

# Questions for Reflection and Discussion

1. What happened in the Garden of Eden to break the fellowship between God and Adam and Eve? Why did sin affect the entire human race?

2. Why did God choose Abraham's descendants? How well have God's chosen people fulfilled God's purpose for them? In what ways do the Jews and their relationship with God represent the entire human race?

3. What is the only remedy for humankind's sin problem? Why is Jesus the only one qualified to pay the penalty for our sin?

4. The Bible contains approximately 2500 prophecies. Of these, more than 2000 have been fulfilled to the letter, and none have been wrong. What does that tell you about the remaining prophecies, which concern the end of the world? Why are so many people in the world betting against the ultimate fulfillment of Bible prophecy?

5. What's the difference between exegesis and hermeneutics? Explain why both are necessary to properly interpret Scripture.

6. What do we mean by "reading Scripture in context"? Give three reasons why reading the Bible in context is crucial.

7. We referred to Bible doctrine several times in this chapter. What is doctrine? (Feel free to use a dictionary). What can happen to a Christian who does not know basic Bible doctrine? What can happen to a Christian who knows incorrect Bible doctrine?

## Moving On...

We hope these last two chapters on the Bible have inspired you to study God's Word more intentionally. The benefits are just too great to miss. Not only does the Bible give you wisdom for living, it gives you much-needed guidance. "Your word is a lamp for my feet and a light for my path," wrote David (Psalm 119:105). Most of all, the Bible directs you to Jesus Christ, who is the theme of the Bible and "the author and perfecter of our faith" (Hebrews 12:2 NIV). The more you study the written Word of God, the more you will get to know the living Word.

Never forget that the Bible is God's way of communicating with you. But how do you communicate with God? That's what the next two chapters are all about.

# Chapter 5

If we conceive of prayer basically as a
means of acquiring things from God,
we trivialize prayer.

*Walter Liefeld*

You make a wish when you blow out the candles on your birthday cake, but you don't really expect your wish will come true. You might have a rabbit's foot on your key chain, but you know it won't bring you good luck. You might even throw a few pennies in the wishing well, but you do it only to get rid of the loose change in your pockets.

Is prayer any different? Do you really expect that something will happen, or is it just a quaint ritual that Christians do without any expectation of results? And even if prayer does work, why should we bother with it? Doesn't God already know what we're going to say? Isn't that what His omniscience is all about?

We're two practical guys, and we're guessing you're that way too. If prayer doesn't do any good, or if it's just repetitive of something God already knows, then let's bag it and use our time for something more productive. One the other hand, if it can make a difference, maybe we ought to get serious about it.

# The Power of
# Prayer

## What's Ahead

- ☐ Why Pray? Because God Says So

- ☐ Pray for a Change

- ☐ Getting Personal with God

- ☐ Praying in God's Will

*Y*ou're going to be disappointed if you turned to this chapter expecting that we'll tell you what words to say in your prayers. (That won't happen until chapter 6—sort of—but don't you dare skip ahead.) Before you start worrying about *what* to say, you should think about *why* you should even bother with praying. After all, if prayer doesn't make a difference to anyone, you could ditch the whole concept and save a few moments out of your busy day.

You may have prayed before for some of the *wrong* concerns:

- You think that's what "good Christians" are supposed to do. (Yes, your saintly grandmother used to do it, but she also used to churn butter and darn her own socks. You don't live in a sod house on the prairie just because she did, so don't pray just because she did.)

- A psychiatrist costs $175 per hour, but God is free. (God may be interested in hearing about your problems, but not if you think of Him only as cheap therapy.)

- You've made a huge mess of your life, and you're yelling at God because you don't want to blame yourself.

- You are desperate for money, and you've got no one else to turn to. (Don't expect to get much from God. He saw you relying on "lady luck" at the casino slot machines before you tried praying.)

- Everyone else at church does it (or at least pretends to), and you don't want any of them to think that you are a spiritual sluggard.

---

*M*any people hope that prayer works so they won't have to.

---

Setting aside the wrong reasons to pray, let's think about the right ones, starting with the single most important reason to pray: God says that we should!

## Why Pray? Because God Says So

God doesn't beat around a burning bush when it comes to prayer. He says that we are to do it! Sometimes the Bible is blunt about it, with verses like this:

*Pray at all times* (Ephesians 6:18).

In other verses, the Bible is a little more flowery:

*Let us come boldly to the throne of our gracious God* (Hebrews 4:16).

Sometimes the Bible verses are instructional:

*One day Jesus told his disciples a story to illustrate their need for constant prayer and to show them that they must never give up* (Luke 18:1).

Other times, we learn the importance of prayer by the example of others, as when the prophet Samuel said this:

> *I will certainly not sin against the L*ORD *by ending my prayers for you* (1 Samuel 12:23).

Often the encouragement to pray is subtly implied by the promised results:

> *The L*ORD *will answer when I call to him* (Psalm 4:3).

But regardless of the style, the mandate is plain and clear:

> *Devote yourselves to prayer* (Colossians 4:2).

The emphasis is so great that it is accurate to say that God *commands* us to pray to Him.

You might ask, "Well, why should I do what God says?" We're quick to answer, "Because He is God, and you aren't!" But beyond the obvious, we'll simply add that God's nature is perfect, so He couldn't ask you to do anything that would be harmful to you. If He commands you to pray, it must be for your own good. So you should do it because He says to, whether you understand the benefits or not.

God doesn't give us any alternative options in this regard. He wants us talking with Him, and He doesn't let us off the hook if we are tired, or if we feel awkward about it, or if we can't think of what to say, or even if things are going fine. All of those factors are irrelevant. He wants us talking with Him—and we have no acceptable excuse for not doing so.

God doesn't ask us to pray just because He is lonesome. (Don't flatter yourself. He's not lonely, and you are not that great of a conversationalist.) God wants you praying because prayer involves Him in your growth as a Christian:

- God's forgiveness of your sins involves prayer.

- Your eternal salvation involves prayer.

- You gain spiritual strength through prayer.

- You are equipped to resist temptation through prayer.

- God may give you wisdom if you pray for it.

- Prayer plays a part in physical healing.

God created everything, so He could have devised any system that He wanted. He chose to use prayer, and you will be missing out on a lot of what He can do for you if you don't get with His program.

## Pray for a Change

If God's *command* that you pray isn't a good enough reason for you (wow, you're tough!), the Bible has another reason that might persuade you: Pray because it works. Things can change if you pray.

### Prayer Changes God

There is an interesting story in the Old Testament about King Hezekiah. He was a good king, but he had a fatal sickness. God's prophet Isaiah came to Hezekiah with these words:

> This is what the LORD says: "Set your affairs in order, for you are going to die. You will not recover from this illness" (2 Kings 20:1).

(Isaiah could have used a little work on his bedside manner.) King Hezekiah wasn't ready to move from the throne to the tomb, but this was in the days before HMOs and life-support systems. So he prayed to God. Back comes Isaiah with a new message from the Lord:

> The LORD...says: "I have heard your prayer....I will heal you....I will add fifteen years to your life" (2 Kings 20:5-6).

So do you think that prayer can change God's mind? Well, we're sure that Hezekiah thought so because he recovered from his illness and lived for 15 more years. (And though the Bible doesn't say so, we believe he bought a lot of life insurance in the fourteenth year.)

Hezekiah isn't the only example of a situation when God "changed His mind." You can see the same principle in other situations:

- God was going to obliterate the Israelites for worshiping the golden calf, but Moses prayed for them to be spared, and God recanted (Deuteronomy 9:7-19).

- God was going to kill Aaron for leading the Israelites astray, but God spared him as the result of Moses' prayer (Deuteronomy 9:20).

- God sent an angel to destroy Jerusalem and its citizens as punishment for King David's sin. Just in the nick of time, David repented and asked God to spare the people of Jerusalem. God relented in response to David's prayer (1 Chronicles 21:14-28).

We don't know how this "changing the mind of God" deal works. Nobody does. But this mystery involves the concept of God knowing everything (being omniscient). Before the world was created, He knew everything that would happen in our lives. He knows what you will be praying about before you even utter the words. So do your prayers really change what God is going to do if He has known all along that He would be doing what you prayed for? See, we told you it was perplexing. But it's a God thing, so don't try to figure it out. You don't have to understand how it works to enjoy the benefit of it (which is the same way we feel about our cars and our computers).

### Prayer Changes Circumstances

Prayer invokes God's involvement in the circumstances of your life. Yes, that's right, you can get God "on your side" through prayer, and He can really make things happen. But don't take our word for it; look at these true-life examples from the Bible:

- Jonah offered a panic prayer as he was getting an inside view of a fish's digestive tract. God caused the fish to regurgitate Jonah on the beach (Jonah 2:7-10).

- Elijah had a "bed and breakfast" arrangement with a widow in Zarephath. When her son died, Elijah asked God to restore the boy's life. That's exactly what happened (1 Kings 17:8-24). And such incidents weren't limited to the Old Testament. The apostle Peter also prayed over a corpse, and the woman came back to life (Acts 9:36-41).

- In what was a cultural disgrace, Hannah couldn't get pregnant. In response to her specific and fervent prayers for a son, God later enabled her to give birth to Samuel, whose name means "heard by God" (1 Samuel 1:1-20).

- This is every weatherman's dream. Elijah predicted a drought, and God made it happen. And it didn't rain again until years later when Elijah prayed for it (1 Kings 17:1; 18:1,41-45).

- On the night before his trial, Peter was in prison, chained between two guards. A prayer meeting was going on for him in the same town. In the middle of the night, an angel appeared in his cell. The chains fell off, and the angel escorted Peter out of the prison without any guards noticing (Acts 12:5-11).

## God Is Not a Lab Rat

Don't get the idea that you can prove the power of prayer in a science-fair demonstration. If you had a test group of 100 people praying for a certain situation, you might come up with zilch. That doesn't mean that God doesn't answer prayers. It just means that He doesn't want to be part of your silly experiment. As we'll discuss later in this chapter, faith plays a big part in prayer. If God's actions could be predicted with the laws of probability, then prayer wouldn't require much faith. God chooses when and what He will do, and He wants you to believe in Him for who He is (not because you think He can be reduced to a mathematical equation or a scientific formula).

You might be praying for God to change your circumstances:

- get you a new job
- smooth out your relationship problems
- cure a health problem
- fix some problems in your family
- solve your financial difficulties

These are the kinds of things that God specializes in, but He likes you to talk to Him about them. Don't get the idea that your problem is too big for God to handle, and don't think that He would consider your request to be trivial or insignificant. If something is important to you, then it is important to God. Notice that Jesus didn't put any boundaries on the types of requests we could make of God:

> *Keep on asking, and you will be given what you ask for* (Matthew 7:7).

### Prayer Changes You

Get ready for things to happen when you pray. Yes, prayer changes things. But most of all, be prepared for your prayers to change *you*, because that is the greatest effect of prayer.

*Prayer brings you into God's presence.* Conversing with God takes you out of your humdrum world and connects you with the Creator of the universe. And that happens immediately. God doesn't have a waiting room where you have to sit for 35 minutes before talking with Him. He does not put you on hold and force you to listen to angel harp-plucking (interrupted by an occasional "Thank you for holding; your call is important to God; please stay on the line, as He answers prayers in the order that they are received"). Nope. When you pray, you are immediately in God's presence, and you've got His undivided attention.

*P*rayer is an interruption of personal ambition.

*Rowland Hogben*

*Prayer changes your attitude and focus.* Let's admit it. We all tend to be self-centered. Even our prayers can be that way. But as we will discuss in the next chapter, our prayers should properly focus on who God is and what He wants to accomplish in our lives. As we pray sincerely, we begin to align ourselves with God's plans rather than our own. We begin to let go of the death grip we have on our own desires, and we begin to subordinate what *we* want for *His* desires. As you pray, you make God the focal point of your life. You change from being self-centered to being God-centered.

## Don't Expect "Presto Change-O"

It's true that God answers prayer. But His answer might not always come immediately. And it might not be the answer you were hoping for. Your timing (usually ASAP) may not be God's timing. So the results that you are praying for may not happen as quickly as you would want them to occur. Also, remember that some of your requests may not happen at all because God knows that what you ask for isn't what's best for you. God always answers prayer. Sometimes His answer is yes, but sometimes He encourages us to be patient, and sometimes the answer is no.

### Getting Personal with God

Immature Christians often make the mistake of treating prayer like rubbing a genie's lamp—they only do it when they want to get something. This is only one of several common misconceptions about prayer.

- Prayer isn't a mystical experience that you enter into by sitting cross-legged while you chant some inane phrase over and over.

- Prayer isn't a formal experience reserved for experts who wear the proper attire (robes are a favorite), stand on elevated platforms in cold buildings, and pray to God on your behalf (as if they were the only ones who can get God's attention).

- Prayer isn't a formal language filled with "thou" and "thee" references that you have to learn, like some secret code.

- Prayer isn't negotiating with God as if you were making some kind of deal: "God, if you do this for me, then I'll do such and such for you."

- Prayer isn't an escape pod that you climb into only when you're in trouble.

Prayer isn't about getting stuff. Many benefits can come to you through prayer, but at its core, the purpose of prayer is to connect you to God.

### Prayer Is Talking with God

You can communicate with someone in many ways, but the best and most effective is talking face-to-face in normal, everyday language, with no pretense, no hidden agendas, and no formality.

The same goes for communicating with God. Even though you can't see God, you can talk to Him *in person,* and the way you do that is through prayer. In the third century, Clement of Alexandria concluded that prayer is "conversation with God," and we would agree. But we also believe that prayer is much more than conversation because God is much more than a person. He is God, and above Him there is no other. No one in heaven or on earth can compare with Him. Therefore, conversing with God is something none of us should take for granted. Prayer is an awesome privilege.

Your growth as a Christian may be helped if you think of God as a king sitting on a throne somewhere in heaven. (Hey, don't laugh. That isn't some childhood fantasy. It's an accurate image of God.) Here's how David—himself a king—envisioned the God that he loved:

> *I lift my eyes to you, O God, enthroned in heaven* (Psalm 123:1)

Okay, so if God is enthroned in heaven, how do we get to Him? Is a huge door standing between the throne room and us? Yes, figuratively speaking, we must open a door, and prayer is the key. Prayer is what gives us access so that we can "come boldly to the throne of our gracious God" (Hebrews 4:16).

But this story of God as King has a twist. The door separating Him and us isn't in His throne room. The door is in our hearts. God doesn't have a door. His throne room is always open. We are the ones who have constructed a barrier between ourselves and the God who made us, who knows us, and who loves us. If our prayers fail to get through to God, it's because our door is closed, not His.

The reason our heart's door is closed is because of sin, which is anything that doesn't meet God's perfect standard (Romans 3:23). The truth is that imperfect people can't come into the presence of a holy God. And if we can't be in His presence, we can't talk to Him.

Many people have this huge misconception that if they simply say, "Hey God, I'm talking to You," they will engage the power of God on their behalf (like rubbing the genie's lamp). This approach is dead wrong. Yes, prayer does engage the power of God, but it doesn't happen when sinful people snap their fingers at God.

### If We Are All Sinners, Who Can Pray?

If sin closes the door of our hearts to God, how can anyone pray? Or, as Dr. James Montgomery Boice writes, "How can I, a sinful human being, approach a holy God?" There's only one way. We have to "get right in God's sight" through the Person of Jesus Christ. The Bible is very clear about this:

> *We are made right in God's sight when we trust in Jesus Christ to take away our sins. And we all can be saved in this same way, no matter who we are or what we have done* (Romans 3:22).

When you became a Christian by accepting Christ as your Savior, Jesus made you right with God. The sacrificial death of Christ washed away your sin and opened your heart's door to allow Christ into your life.

> *Look! Here I stand at the door and knock. If you hear me calling and open the door, I will come in, and we will share a meal as friends* (Revelation 3:20).

Make no mistake about it. When you believed by faith that God saved you because of what Jesus did for you (Romans 5:1), you were saved—forever. Nothing and no one can separate you from the awesome power of God's love (Romans 8:38).

But let's admit it. You are still an imperfect person. All Christians are. We have been justified (made right) in God's sight, but we are still imperfect because our new spiritual nature struggles against our old sinful nature. That struggle is, as the apostle Paul called it, a "fact of life" for the believer. Can you identify with Paul?

> *It seems to be a fact of life that when I want to do what is right, I inevitably do what's wrong. I love God's law with all my heart. But there is another law at work within me that is at war with my mind. . . . So you see how it is: In my mind I really want to obey God's law, but because of my sinful nature I am a slave to sin* (Romans 7:21-25).

Can you relate? You want to please God with your actions, but you occasionally slip back into some old sinful habits. That should occur less and less as you grow as a Christian. But you hate it when that happens—and so does God. He continues to love you, but He hates your sin.

You don't lose your salvation when you sin, but your sins certainly interfere with your ability to communicate with God. Remember, He can't be in the presence of sin. To follow our analogy, you've slammed the door of your heart in His face. Here is how the prophet Isaiah explained the concept to the Israelites who loved God but continued to keep sinning:

> Listen! The LORD is not too weak to save you, and he is not becoming deaf. He can hear you when you call. But there is a problem—your sins have cut you off from God. Because of your sin, he has turned away and will not listen anymore (Isaiah 59:1-2).

But you can easily reopen the door and restore your communication with God. All it takes is *confession*.

### Confession: Don't Let Sin Get in Your Way

You confessed your sins when you accepted Christ as your Savior. That confession was part of the salvation process. Now we are talking about keeping the door of your heart open to God with an ongoing attitude of confession for sins as you commit them. If you aren't sorry for the sins you commit, and if you refuse to confess them to God, you are living in spiritual arrogance and defiance of God. As a holy God, He can't have fellowship with you when you're rebellious like that.

Confession isn't just good for your conscience. It opens your heart's door so that you can once again come into the presence of God.

> If I had not confessed the sin in my heart, my Lord would not have listened. But God did listen! He paid attention to my prayer. Praise God, who did not ignore my prayer and did not withdraw his unfailing love from me (Psalm 66:18-20).

Remember, prayer is a conversation between you and your heavenly Father who loves you. In any relationship between two people who love each other, if one fouls up and offends the other, they can't enjoy intimate conversation between them until the situation is rectified.

After you sin, go to God in prayer. The first words you say to Him don't have to be your confession (you might want to start by praising Him for His loving and forgiving character). But sometime soon in the conversation you should get to your confession and apology. With that relationship restored, you're back on track to grow more in your faith.

## Praying in God's Will

You might be skeptical if we told you that you can pray for anything. It sounds too good to be true. What about selfish motivations or praying for things that God doesn't really want for us? Well, you're right to be skeptical, because the statement has a condition that goes along with it: *You can pray for anything as long as you are praying within God's will.*

God is sovereign. That means He is in control of all that happens in the universe, and everything is subject to His grand design. God wants us to be impressed with that reality when we pray. We can pray for results that seem appropriate to us (from our limited perspective), but the requests of our prayers need to acknowledge that we want His will to be accomplished. Simply stated: God wants us to pray in accordance with His will.

> *And we can be confident that he will listen to us whenever we ask him for anything in line with his will* (1 John 5:14).

Even Jesus prayed according to His Father with this condition in place: "Yet I want your will, not mine" (Matthew 26:39).

Our prayers should be made in a context something like this: "Well, God, those are the things that I'm worried about and the outcomes that I'd like to see. But You know everything. You know what is best for me, and I trust You with the outcome in my life. So, in the final analysis, I really want what You want for my life. Don't give me what I ask for if You don't want me to have it. I ask that You give to me what You know I need."

*H*ow are you supposed to know what God's will is when you pray? We cover the subject of knowing God's will for your life in chapters 11 and 12.

### Prayer and Desire

So these are the two conditions of prayer:

- confessing your sins and completely opening your heart's door to God, and

- praying according to God's will for your life, not your own selfish motivations.

When you fulfill these two conditions, something wonderful happens. The desires of your heart match up with God's desires. You literally become a person with a heart for God. This is the place where God wants you. This is where He can use you. To have a heart for God means that you are tuned in to His frequency. The communication channel between you and God is crystal clear. When you pray, God listens. When He speaks, you can hear Him.

You don't have to be perfect to have a heart for God. The Bible says that King David—despite his rather huge failings and weaknesses—was a man after God's own heart. That's why David was able to write this:

> Take delight in the LORD, *and he will give you your heart's desires* (Psalm 37:4).

Can you imagine being so connected to God that you delight in conversing with Him? Can you imagine that as you pray, God will change the motivations of your heart so that they match His plans for your life? All of a sudden, prayer doesn't seem so boring, does it?

*P*rayer is no fitful, short-lived thing. It is no voice crying unheard and unheeded in the silence. It is a voice that goes into God's ear.

*E.M. Bounds*

# What's That Again?

1. Don't get caught in a trap of praying for the wrong reasons. You can't expect to be enthusiastic about prayer unless you believe that it really makes a difference.

2. Above everything else, you should pray because God tells us to.

3. Prayer is part of the process that God uses to work in our lives. Prayer changes a lot of things, but it is most likely to change you. It brings you into God's plan (not the other way around).

4. Prayer is simply talking with a personal God who loves you and knows you and knows what is best for you.

5. Your prayers must include confession of your sins. Although your sins were forgiven when you accepted Christ as your Savior, you need to confess the sins you've committed so you have an open line of communication with God.

6. You can pray for anything when you are praying within the context of God's will for your life. All of your requests need to be subject to God's overriding judgment and knowledge for what is best for you.

## Dig Deeper

Here are some classic books on prayer:

*Praying to the God You Can Trust* by Leith Anderson. The subtitle aptly describes the subject of the book: *Discovering the God of Hope When Prayer Doesn't Seem to Change Things.*

*Prayer: The Great Adventure* by David Jeremiah. This is a great book covering the basics of prayer, including the whys and the hows, that lead to the adventure of knowing God.

*All Things Are Possible Through Prayer* by Charles L. Allen. Practical and easy-to-read, this book is filled with true stories about the effects of prayer.

*How to Pray* by R.A. Torrey. A true classic, and only 100 pages long. Dr. Torrey lists 11 reasons why prayer is important.

*E.M. Bounds on Prayer* by E.M. Bounds. This one-volume collection includes seven books by the man who has written more about prayer than anyone else.

# $\mathcal{Q}$uestions for $\mathcal{R}$eflection and $\mathcal{D}$iscussion

1. Why does God want us to talk with Him? He already knows what's going on in our lives, so He doesn't need information. What other reasons could there be?

2. Do you agree that prayer "brings you into God's presence"? Do you notice any change in your feelings or attitudes when you pray?

3. If you were talking to God right now, what circumstances in your life would you want Him to change? What is it about *you* that you would want God to change? What is it about you that God might want to change?

4. What do you think God does with "desperate" prayers? These are the prayers offered by people who are in frantic situations. Does it make any difference if the person praying has or hasn't opened his or her heart's door to Jesus?

5. What does "praying in the will of God" mean?

6. Give an example of praying outside the will of God.

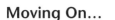

## Moving On...

When praying is a new experience for you, it may seem awkward. As with any "first time" experience, you aren't exactly sure what you should be doing. People can tell you to relax and "just talk to God," but you might have lots of questions: Are your hands supposed to be folded or raised in the air? Are your eyes supposed to be open or closed? Is prayer more effective in the morning or the evening? And should your prayers rhyme (or at least be spoken in Shakespearean English)?

In the next chapter, we'll cover some of the "how to" specifics of prayer. With that orientation, we're sure that you can relax and move into a prayer life that is natural, comfortable, and awesome.

There's something in the next chapter for you even if you've been praying for a long time. For people in that category, praying often becomes routine. While they don't want to admit it, praying seems a little boring to them after the newness has worn off. Nobody likes prayer when it gets to that stage—especially God. That's why the next chapter introduces some ways in which you can energize your prayer life.

Whether you are new to talking with God or have been at it for a long while, God wants your conversations with Him to be dynamic and exciting. He wants prayer to be the highlight of your day. And that's exactly what it can become.

# Chapter 6

I may use the most beautiful words and
phrases, but until I am connected with the
Great Source of power, my prayers are just
meaningless words.

*Charles L. Allen*

Do you feel like a spiritual weakling? Do you wish you could experience power and passion in your Christian life? An effective prayer life may be just what you need.

In chapter 5, we talked about *why* to pray (because God said to and because it works). And we discussed that prayer is simply talking to God, beginning with getting right with Him and then getting aligned with His will. With those principles covered, now you're ready for an exercise program for your prayer life. Just like physical exercise increases your physical stamina and overall health, prayer will do wonders for your overall spiritual life.

"But wait!" you may be saying. You need more than *principles* about prayer. You're also curious about some of the *logistics* of prayer:

- What are you going to say? You can ask for stuff, but should you start off with that? Maybe it would be better to begin with a few thanksgiving-type phrases. Are there subjects you should avoid, like politics or sex?

- And how are you going to say it? Do you have to sound like the King James Version of the Bible?

- And should you be standing or sitting...or maybe even kneeling (which seems like a religious thing to do)?

Those are honest questions, and we've got a great place to look for the answers.

# What to Say
# When You Pray

*H*ave you ever had an experience that left you speechless, not knowing what to say? Maybe you tried to say something—you even opened your mouth and moved your jaw—but nothing came out. It seems to happen in situations like these:

- You split the seam in the seat of your pants on the playground in the fourth grade.

- The highway patrol officer asks if you know how fast you were driving.

- You open your wallet after dinner in a restaurant and see nothing but lint.

And number one on everyone's speechless list would be this: trying to talk to God for the first time.

But don't worry if you've tried praying and the only noises that came out of your mouth were guttural grunts that sounded like you had a clogged trachea. It really isn't that hard once you know what to pray about and what to say. As a matter of fact, it's as easy as...talking.

## Jesus Knew What He Was Praying About

Jesus understood that all of us would have difficulty talking to God unless we knew what we were supposed to say. To help us out, He gave a sample prayer to His disciples in Matthew 6:9-13. You might recognize it best in the old-fashioned King James Version of the Bible:

> *After this manner therefore pray ye: Our Father which art in heaven, hallowed be thy name. Thy kingdom come. Thy will be done in earth, as it is in heaven. Give us this day our daily bread. And forgive us our debts, as we forgive our debtors. And lead us not into temptation, but deliver us from evil: For thine is the kingdom, and the power, and the glory, for ever. Amen.*

This sample prayer is usually referred to as the Lord's Prayer. You can find it printed on laminated wall plaques, on bookmarks, and sometimes on the back of a postage stamp (usually written by some calligrapher who has a magnifying glass and strained eyesight).

We thought studying the components of the Lord's Prayer would be instructive. After all, it was the pattern that Jesus told us to follow. But as poetic as the King James Version sounds, we think studying the Lord's Prayer in a more modern version would be helpful. Here is how it reads in the New Living Translation:

> *Pray like this: Our Father in heaven, may your name be honored. May your Kingdom come soon. May your will be done here on earth, just as it is in heaven. Give us our food for today, and forgive us our sins, just as we have forgiven those who have sinned against us. And don't let us yield to temptation, but deliver us from the evil one. For yours is the kingdom and the power and the glory forever. Amen.*

### Follow the Pattern

Let's dissect this prayer and see what we can learn about how we should talk to God:

- *Our Father:* It is always good to start off our prayer by reminding ourselves of our personal relationship to God. He is our heavenly Father, and He loves us because we are His own spiritual children.

- *In heaven:* We need to remind ourselves of God's majesty, that He is in control of the universe, and that nothing is too difficult for Him.

- *May your name be honored:* We shouldn't be hollering at God like we would at a peanut vendor at a baseball game. He is worthy of our respect and devotion. Our praise to Him is appropriate because of who He is, and it keeps us in the right frame of mind.

- *May your Kingdom come soon:* Christ is going to come back to earth someday, and He will rule over it. Remembering this fact will chisel some of the arrogance out of our lives.

- *May your will be done here on earth, just as it is in heaven:* We need to adopt God's priorities as our own. He should be the primary influence in our personal life, in our family life, on the job, and in whatever we do.

- *Give us our food for today:* God wants us to be asking Him for the things that we need and want. (If we are praying in His will, then we'll be asking for the things He might already want us to have.)

- *And forgive us our sins:* In chapter 5, we talked about keeping the door of our heart open to God by confessing our sins. Sin interrupts the conversation we can have with Him, so it is important to always keep the line of communication free from "sin static."

- *Just as we have forgiven those who have sinned against us:* Wait a minute—this is getting too personal! But hey, we're talking to a very personal God. He wants us to be praying about our relationships and how we treat other people.

- *And don't let us yield to temptation, but deliver us from the evil one:* We should pray that God will help us overcome (and avoid) those circumstances that tempt us to sin. We live at the center of spiritual warfare, and we want God on our side.

- *For yours is the kingdom and the power and the glory forever:* The prayer ends the same way that it begins—praising God. Isn't it amazing that God cares for us and that He wants us talking to Him? Don't forget to tell Him that you appreciate that privilege.

## Should You Say "Amen" Even If You Aren't a Baptist?

There is nothing magic about the word *amen*. It means "let it be so." It's a traditional sign-off for prayers, but it's not required. You could just say, "That's all for now," and God wouldn't be offended.

Look at the different categories that this one prayer covers:

- praise (acknowledging God's importance in our lives)
- priorities (wanting His will instead of our own)
- provision (asking for what we need)
- personal relationships (talking about how we interact with other people)
- protection (asking for help to live a godly and moral life)

Your prayers don't have to be any different or any more complicated. Just talk to God about these kinds of things.

## Be Yourself

Notice that Christ gave us examples of *what* to talk about, but He didn't tell us *how* to say it. That means you might have some lingering questions:

- What language does God speak?

- Does He prefer formality?

- Or can we be casual?

If those are your questions, here are the answers: "All of them," "Not unless you prefer it," and "Yes." Do you get the point? God has been listening to prayers for thousands of years. During that time, people have been praying in a lot of different languages and a lot of different styles. They have prayed while they were mad and happy and scared and thoughtful (although not usually with all of those emotions at the same time). God wants us to pray the way we feel.

### Sounds Like...

Have you ever heard your voice played back on a tape recorder? It sounds weird to you, doesn't it? Do you worry about how your voice should sound when you pray to God? Well, don't. God doesn't care if you speak with a Shakespearean accent or with a Southern drawl. He doesn't even care if your words are audible. He can hear what you are thinking in your head, so you've got your choice:

- Option 1: Pray silently in your mind.

- Option 2: Talk to God out loud.

- Option 3: Pray silently but with your lips still moving (you know, like some people do when they are reading).

### Praying with Body Language

By this point, you might feel a little more confident about what your mouth should be saying during your prayers. But what about the rest of your body? If you went to Sunday school when you were a little kid, maybe you feel compelled to close your eyes and fold your hands. Well, that's not mandatory (it was just your teacher's trick to keep your hands to yourself during prayer time). Actually, the Bible describes people praying with all sorts of body language.

For example, as far as your *prayer posture* is concerned, your options are unlimited:

- *Standing:* In many cultures, people customarily stand in the presence of royalty. Standing during your prayer time can remind you of the respect that God deserves.

- *Sitting:* If you're reading your Bible at your desk, God will be mighty glad if you start praying right there.

- *Kneeling:* This position acknowledges our humility in God's presence.

- *Lying on your back:* Psalm 63:6 mentions praying while lying awake in bed. It is certainly comfortable, but you might find the "lying awake" part to be difficult if you delay praying until Letterman or Leno are over.

- *Lying facedown on the ground:* In the cultures during Bible times, this was a position of repentance. Personally, it is not our favorite prayer position (because we find it a little hard on the nose).

And you have options for your *hands* as well:

- *Hands folded:* Many people prefer to pray this way, and you see it in a lot of religious pictures.

- *Hands raised:* This is a posture of surrender or of worship. It is usually done with the palms up.

- *Hands in your pockets:* We see this a lot at church when people are standing in prayer. Actually, this is never mentioned in the Bible, but that is because the Bible was written before pants were invented.

Your options for your eyes are more limited, but that is a physiological restriction, not a spiritual one. You've only got two choices, but either one is fine with God:

- *Eyes closed:* Nothing is particularly religious or holy about closing your eyes. It just helps you keep your thoughts focused on God.

- *Eyes open:* This is the preferred way if you happen to be praying while you're driving.

We hope you get the point here. There is no right or wrong posture for prayer. God is more interested in the attitude of your heart than the position of your body. This means that you've got the freedom to experiment a little bit so you don't get in a prayer rut.

## Shut Up and Listen

Notice that we have been referring to prayer as talking *with* God—not talking *to* God. Prayer is a two-way conversation. We do some of the talking while God listens. But then we need to let God do some of the talking while we listen.

At this point you might be thinking that we've lost our last shreds of sanity. Well, let us explain. When we refer to letting God talk, we don't expect that you will be hearing little angel voices in your head. We don't even think that you will hear God using His best James Earl Jones impression with a deep bass voice booming down from heaven.

God is most likely to speak to you in the quietness of your thoughts. As you pray in His will, you are going to get a sense of what He wants. He will speak to you by prompting your thoughts.

In your prayer time, you should leave time for God to talk to you. Let Him have His turn. God has even said that you should shut up for a while and listen for Him (only He said it a little more tactfully):

*Be silent, and know that I am God* (Psalm 46:10).

### Putting Words in Your Mouth

What if you want to pray about a situation but don't know what to ask for? What if you are going through a difficult time and just can't explain it? Maybe you are so sad or emotionally distraught that you can't articulate your feelings. What if you want to pray for God's will but don't know what it is?

This would be a great time to shut up and listen because God is ready to put words in your mouth—literally. People who have a personal relationship with God have the Holy Spirit alive within them. One of the jobs of the Holy Spirit is to pray on our behalf when we don't know what to say.

> *And the Holy Spirit helps us in our distress. For we don't even know what we should pray for, nor how we should pray. But the Holy Spirit prays for us with groanings that cannot be expressed in words. And the Father who knows all hearts knows what the Spirit is saying, for the Spirit pleads for us believers in harmony with God's own will* (Romans 8:26-27).

If you find yourself in this situation, just be silent and hang in there. Tell God that you don't know how you should be praying and that you'll be quiet so that the Holy Spirit can do the praying for you.

## Use the Force

E.M. Bounds, who has written more about prayer than anyone, called prayer "the force that shapes the world." He also wrote this:

> The prayers of God's saints are the capital stock in heaven by which Christ carries on His great work upon the earth. Great throes and mighty convulsions in the world have come about as a result of these prayers. The earth is changed, revolutionized; angels move on more powerful, more rapid wings; and God's policy is shaped when the prayers of His people are more numerous and more efficient.

Do you believe that? Do you believe your prayers have the potential of moving the hand of God? You better believe it because prayer is a force of unimaginable dimension. This is no namby-pamby Obi-Wan Kenobi force from the fiction of George Lucas' films. Prayer is the greatest force in the world, and it is available to you.

### Praying with Power

Walking around with Jesus must have been a kick for the disciples. He was always coming up with wild stuff that must have left them scratching their heads. For instance, listen to this:

> *Have faith in God. I assure you that you can say to this mountain, "May God lift you up and throw you into the sea," and your command will be obeyed. All that's required is that you really believe and do not doubt in your heart* (Mark 11:22-23).

The Bible doesn't say how Jesus' followers responded to His statement about moving mountains by the power of prayer, but they must have been a little skeptical. Aren't you?

Did Jesus really mean you could literally move a mountain just by praying? Of course not. Jesus was fond of using figurative language to drive home a point. His point here is that moving a mountain would appear to be an impossible task. Yet that's exactly what God is capable of doing when we pray—the impossible.

Do you have an impossible task facing you right now? God can handle it. Is there something overwhelming in your future? Give it to God. When you get to the point where human effort has no effect, that's where God can work. For future reference, memorize these words from Jesus:

> *Humanly speaking, it is impossible. But with God everything is possible* (Matthew 19:26).

When you truly believe that God can do the impossible, pray with an open heart in God's will, and God will answer. That's mountain-moving prayer.

### Praying with Faith

Pastor Bill Hybels gives two principles for building and praying with a faith that moves mountains:

- *Faith comes from looking at God, not at the mountain.* When an impossible situation faces you, it's tempting to look at the mountain. We become like Peter when he was walking on the water (Matthew 14:25-32). He was doing fine as long as he kept his eyes on Jesus, but as soon as he looked around and focused on the waves, he began to sink. When you pray, keep your eyes on the size of your great Lord; to Him, your insurmountable mountain is just a molehill.

- *God gives us faith as we walk with Him.* Your faith is like a muscle. If you don't exercise it, your faith grows weak. But if you use it every day, your faith will grow strong because God will add to it. Don't shy away from praying about those mountains that need to be moved. Keep at it with the confident assurance that God is able and will intervene on your behalf (either in the way you are praying or in an even better way).

### Praying with Purpose

As your faith muscle grows, the force of your prayers will grow stronger as well. You'll find yourself becoming a prayer superhero! Actually, the traditional description is more like a prayer *warrior*. History is filled with the stories of faithful saints who prayed tirelessly for God to move in the lives of individuals, neighborhoods, nations, and the world. A prayer warrior has probably prayed for you, whether you know it or not!

You really don't have to be a superhero to be a prayer warrior. Any ordinary person will do. You just have to be faithful to God and His Word. God desires to do mighty things in you, your neighborhood, your nation, and your world. But He needs you to pray! Here is what E.M. Bounds said about this:

Men and women are needed whose prayers will give to the world the utmost power of God, whose prayers will make His promises blossom with rich and full results. God is waiting to hear us, and He challenges us to pray that He might work.

If you want to pray with purpose, you need to be deliberate and specific. Here are some suggestions of the things that you can be praying for:

1. *Pray for others.* "People must pray, and people must be prayed for," wrote Bounds. You can pray for anything you want, but people should be at the top of your list. Pray for people who are hurting, people who are confused about spiritual matters, people who are lonely, and people who don't think they need God. Ask God to give you a heart for people. Loners become team players in the body of Christ. And when you pray for people, don't pray in general terms, like the classic, "Lord, we pray for all the missionaries in the foreign lands." When you pray with purpose, you pray for people by name.

2. *Pray for the lost.* Do you sometimes get frustrated with the way people openly reject Jesus? Pray! Our hearts should break over people whose eternal destinies are without hope. We have the answer, and we need to tell others. But before we can say a thing, we need to pray. Evelyn Christenson writes, "In pre-evangelism praying, we ask the omnipotent God of the universe to reach down and work in people's lives *before* we do. And what a difference such praying makes!"

3. *Pray for healing.* Medical science has made tremendous advancements in health and disease control. Today our life expectancy is twice what it was 100 years ago. Yet sickness is everywhere, from temporary ailments to illnesses without cures. Whether you are sick or someone you know is suffering, your first response should be to pray with purpose and faith, for God is the God who heals (Exodus 15:26). Charles Allen lists these four steps to gain healing and health through faith and prayer:

A.  Believe that God can and will heal.

B.  Believe that God can use medical science to accomplish His purposes.

C.  Remove all "spiritual hindrances" to healing, such as sin and wrong attitudes.

D.  Accept God's will for your life.

*4. Pray for peace of mind.* Is there anything more desirable in the world than peace of mind? Everyone wants it, yet few people know how to get it. Hey, it's not as complicated as people think. Our experience has been that the surest way to peace of mind is through prayer.

> *You will keep in perfect peace all who trust in you, whose thoughts are fixed on you!* (Isaiah 26:3).

People worry about so many things, and yet we can do only one thing for peace of mind. We need to pray and believe that God will supply all our needs and ease our mind.

> *Trust in the Lord with all your heart; do not depend on your own understanding. Seek his will in all you do, and he will direct your paths* (Proverbs 3:5-6).

*5. Pray for confidence in the future.* People seem to worry most about the future, don't they? What's going to happen? What will we do? How will we ever get through such and such? Where will we go? What if…? The future can be a scary place, and there's only one thing you can do to gain confidence for what lies ahead: Pray to God who knows the future. People sometimes say, "I don't know what the future holds, but I know who holds the future." That's a powerful statement. We can have confidence in the future because we can have confidence in God. Don't pray to know what the future holds (God probably won't tell you anyway), but pray for the confidence to handle whatever happens. God doesn't promise to take away potential problems, but He will equip you to handle them.

*6. Pray for repentance.* The first step in giving your life to Christ is repentance. To repent means to go in the opposite direction. God saves by His grace (Ephesians 2:8-9), but you must willingly turn your back on sin. As we previously discussed in chapter 5, once God saves you, you're saved forever and it doesn't wear off. But you still have the capacity to sin. All Christians do. That's why we need to keep walking away from sin. We still need to repent. A key part of praying with purpose is praying for repentance—for yourself and for your fellow believers. Sin will drag us down; repentance puts us back in line with God's agenda. Evelyn Christenson writes that repentance involves several steps. First, we must admit that our wrongdoings are sin (as opposed to "mistakes" or "errors in judgment"). Secondly, we need to recognize that our sins offend a holy God; we can't take them lightly. Thirdly, we must confess our sins to God in prayer and ask for forgiveness. The final step involves turning away from our sin. Every step involves prayer.

*7. Pray for revival.* An amazing thing happens when God's people pray and seek the Lord and turn away from sin. Read it for yourself:

> *Then if my people who are called by my name will humble themselves and pray and seek my face and turn from their wicked ways, I will hear from heaven and will forgive their sins and heal their land* (2 Chronicles 7:14).

God promises to heal the land where His people live. So many times we blame our political leaders or the culture for the negative things going on in our nation. We tend to believe that conditions in the world will get better only if people without the Lord turn to Him. Yes, we should pray for that to happen. But even more importantly, we need to pray that God's people will turn back to God. Read that verse again. It's the prayers of God's people that move God to heal our land, not the prayers of pagans. And when God's people pray with purpose, revival comes.

### Praying with Passion

When we pray with *power*, we're asking God to handle the impossible. When we pray with *faith*, we're confident that He will do it. When we pray with *purpose*, we get very specific about who and what we pray for. But there's another step that's involved in the force of prayer—praying with *passion*.

When you are passionate about someone or something, you have very strong feelings. You get emotional. That's the way you need to approach your prayer life. Put some feeling into it! Don't just give God lip service. Pour your heart into your prayers.

### Intercessory Prayer

You will be most passionate when you pray for other people. The theological term for this is *intercession*. Here's what it means. When you pray for other people, you literally plead to God on their behalf. That's what it means to intercede. The Bible is full of people who pleaded to God on behalf of others:

- Abraham interceded on behalf of his nephew Lot, and God listened (Genesis 18:16-33).

- Moses prayed to God on behalf of the people of Israel (this happened often), and God heard him (Numbers 11:1-2).

- Elijah pleaded with God to prove Himself to the people of Israel and the pagan prophets, and God answered (1 Kings 18:36-37).

And here's the real kicker. Jesus is interceding for us right now!

> *Who then will condemn us? Will Christ Jesus? No, for he is the one who died for us and was raised to life for us and is sitting at the place of highest honor next to God, pleading for us* (Romans 8:34).

Isn't that incredible? The Son of God, our Savior, didn't pray to God just when He was on earth. He is praying—He is pleading—to God right now, and He's doing it for us. This should humble us and motivate us to pray for other people, regardless of who they are.

> *I urge you, first of all, to pray for all people. As you make your requests, plead for God's mercy upon them, and give thanks* (1 Timothy 2:1).

## Persistence Prays

You would think that we could pray for something once, and...boom. God's got it. We don't like it when people nag us about stuff, so we figure, *Hey, God heard me. He's not deaf. I won't bother Him again with this request.*

No, God isn't deaf, but He does like to hear things more than once. No, He's not forgetful, but He wants us to keep talking with Him. (Perhaps it has something to do with what we talked about in chapter 5—prayer changes *us*). Think of it this way. What if someone you care about very much were to say to you, "You are the greatest—there's no one like you." You would never respond by saying, "Thanks for the compliment, but never say that to me again." Instead, you would be inclined to say, "You know, I'm not sure I heard you correctly. Could you repeat that?"

We're stretching things a bit, but that's the way God is. He hears our prayers, and He loves our prayers. In fact, He loves them so much that He wants us to live in a continual state of prayer:

> *Keep on praying* (1 Thessalonians 5:17).

And if you don't think God is influenced by persistent prayers, think again. The Bible says that God rewards those who "diligently seek him" (Hebrews 11:6 KJV). It's always in our best interest to pray with persistence.

### Be Patient

We're coming to the end of our discussion of prayer, and we've deliberately saved one of the most important principles of prayer for the end. Are you ready? Here it is:

> *When you pray, wait patiently for God.*

Waiting on the Lord is one of the hardest things you will ever do as a Christian. We want things and we want them now, but that's just not how God operates. We think our prayers go unanswered, but that's because our perspective is so limited. If only we could see with God's eyes and feel with God's heart. Then we would know how much He loves us, how much He wants for us, and how much He wants us to trust Him.

We need to trust that God will answer every prayer in the proper time and for our absolute good. We may not understand that now. We may never understand why God says yes to some things and no to others. But we can always trust Him to do the right thing. Here's how Leith Anderson says it:

> To trust God is to put all of our weight on him. When we don't understand, when we hurt, when we suffer disappointment, when we are past asking for something or someone, when we feel furious over the outcome—then trusting God is finally just collapsing in exhaustion on him. That is when prayer comes back to its purest meaning of communion. When we are on the other side of asking we simply come to God for who he is and connect with him in the most basic expression of faith.

# What's That Again?

1. The Lord's Prayer is a good pattern for us to follow, but we don't need to copy it verbatim. Our prayers should include elements of praising God, thanking God, and asking God.

2. There is no single correct style for praying. Just be yourself and talk with God about what is on your heart. But prayer is a two-way conversation, so give God time to speak to you.

3. You can pray in lots of different ways. They are all acceptable, and you can change your style as it seems appropriate to you. God is more concerned about the condition of your heart than the position of your body.

4. Prayer is a mighty force. You'll see the results of that force as you pray with power, faith, purpose, and passion.

5. Praying with persistence is a key to success with God. Being patient in your praying means that you trust God (and trust His timetable for whatever you are praying about).

## Dig Deeper

You don't have to be an experienced artist to do something artistic. (Just look at the refrigerator door of any mother with a preschooler.) With a little practice, your artistic skills can improve. Well, praying is an art form too. And here are a few books that can give you some excellent pointers as you practice talking with God.

> *A Life of Prayer*, Paul Cedar. This book starts with the request the disciples asked of Jesus: "Lord, teach us to pray." It gives insightful suggestions and instructions.

> *Too Busy Not to Pray*, Bill Hybels. This book starts with a great title and gets better after that. Written by the pastor of one of America's largest churches, it will help you find time to pray.

> *Let Prayer Change Your Life*, Becky Tirabassi. Becky conducts group workshops on prayer. This book contains some practical pointers about keeping a prayer notebook.

*Praying God's Way*, Evelyn Christenson. We found this book to be very helpful in the area of learning how to pray for others, especially the unsaved. Christenson has been very involved in the AD2000 Lighthouse Movement, an international prayer effort.

*Desperate for God*, Nancie Carmichael. This book will inspire you to turn your whole heart to God. Our goal should be to mature in our prayer life so that we are desperate for a deeper relationship with Him.

# $\mathcal{Q}$uestions for $\mathcal{R}$eflection and $\mathcal{D}$iscussion

1. Describe the content of your typical prayer. Do you have a pattern that you follow, or maybe a checklist, or do you use the "as the Spirit leads" technique?

2. Review the Lord's Prayer. Take each phrase and describe, in your own words, the types of things Jesus was praying about.

3. How does God speak to you? Are you listening for Him? What method do you use in your prayer time to give God a turn to talk?

4. What's the "body language" that you use most often when you pray? Have you tried other ways to pray? If so, does one form work better than another? If not, what's keeping you from experimenting?

5. Give an example of something "impossible" you prayed for. What were the results?

6. Who are the people you are most concerned about right now? What worries you the most? Make a list and commit to pray for those people and things every day for the next week. At the end of the week, see what God has done with your list.

7. What's more difficult for you—*persistence* in prayer or *patience* in prayer?

## Moving On...

Many new Christians have some apprehensions when they are talking to God. But they often get even more tongue-tied when they try to share their faith with other people. What if you get asked a question you can't answer? What if the person you are talking to is skeptical, or even worse, is antagonistic toward Christianity? Maybe it is just better—at least safer—if you keep your opinions about your faith to yourself.

We know your fears. We've had the same ones. But think about this for a minute. If everyone kept their excitement about the Christian faith to themselves, no one would have shared the truth of Jesus with you. You've got a life-changing message happening inside of you, and Jesus wants you to tell others about it.

In the next couple of chapters we'll discuss the sometimes dreaded concept of *witnessing*. As you're about to see, it is actually very exciting. And we're guessing that by the time you've read chapters 7 and 8, you won't be able to keep your mouth shut about Christ.

# Chapter 7

There is no nobler calling, no better investment of one's life, than telling others how to know God personally and enjoy Him forever.

*Bill Bright*

Living the Christian life is both the easiest and the hardest thing you'll ever do. It's easy because there's nothing you can do to earn God's special favor. You can't apply to become a Christian, and you don't qualify anyway. But God loves you because He is God, and He saves you because of Jesus Christ. Once you give your life to Jesus, your eternal future is secure.

The Christian life is also hard because God doesn't want you to just sit there and wait for heaven. He's asked you to do certain things, the most important of which is to tell others about what He has done for you. That's what sharing your faith is all about, and that's what the next two chapters are all about. Sharing your faith should be the most natural thing in the world. But it's often very difficult, mainly because we don't really understand it.

By the end of this chapter, we hope you do understand what it means to share your faith, and we pray that you will be ready to take the next step.

# Sharing Your Faith
# Is Not Optional

## $\mathcal{W}$hat's $\mathcal{A}$head

- ☐ The Greatest Gift in the World

- ☐ What Does Sharing Your Faith Mean?

- ☐ The Method to God's Plan

- ☐ The Great Commission

- ☐ You've Got All the Help You Need

- ☐ Know What You Believe

*W*hat's the greatest gift you ever received? It certainly wasn't that belt sander your husband gave you for your anniversary, or the extra large bottle of mouthwash your friends wrapped up for your last birthday. Your most memorable gift was probably something like that red bike you got for Christmas as a kid, or the car your dad gave you for graduation. Or maybe it was a bouquet of flowers sent by someone very special.

When you receive an unexpected and truly wonderful gift, you experience a whole range of emotions. You are surprised, delighted, and grateful as you look at and think about this thoughtful thing someone has done for you. And then, once you settle down and realize exactly what you have, you are compelled to tell someone—anyone. You tell your family, you call your friends, and you even show off your gift to perfect strangers. It's all part of the experience of receiving a great gift.

## The Greatest Gift in the World

You could stack up all the terrific gifts you have received in your lifetime. In fact, you could collect all the great gifts ever given to people everywhere for all time, and they wouldn't begin to compare to the single greatest gift in the world, given to you by the God of the universe—the gift of salvation.

> *God saved you by his special favor when you believed. And you can't take credit for this; it is a gift from God* (Ephesians 2:8).

### What Is Salvation?

For the Christian, salvation is literally the act of being saved from sin. All of us have sinned and fall short of God's glorious standard (Romans 3:23), and the result of that sin is physical and spiritual death (Romans 6:23). We can't save ourselves from death; only God is capable, and only God is willing to save us. The way He has chosen to save us is through Jesus (Ephesians 1:9). There is no other way to get right with God (John 14:6). That's why the Bible says this about salvation and Jesus:

> *There is salvation in no one else! There is no other name in all of heaven for people to call on to save them* (Acts 4:12).

### Salvation Is a Gift, Not a Secret

The qualities of your salvation are very much like the qualities of a gift—

- A gift always has benefits.

- A gift suggests a personal connection between the giver and the receiver.

- When you receive a gift, you naturally want to share it with others.

On the other hand, salvation and secrecy have nothing in common—

- Few secrets have benefits.
- The person who told you the secret rarely has a personal connection with the secret itself.
- When someone tells you a secret, you're supposed to keep it to yourself.

Yet many people treat salvation as if it's some kind of secret. They know what a wonderful thing they have, but they're reluctant to tell others. They may even be afraid. Why do you think this happens? We think it has to do with a misunderstanding of what it means to share your faith.

## What Does Sharing Your Faith Mean?

The phrase that we're using in this book to describe the process of talking about God and receiving the gift of salvation is *sharing your faith*. The Bible never actually uses that phrase. Instead, the Bible uses words like these:

- *Witness*—"You will receive power when the Holy Spirit comes on you; and you will be my witnesses in Jerusalem, and in all Judea and Samaria, and to the ends of the earth" (Acts 1:8 NIV).

- *Evangelize*—"He is the one who gave these gifts to the church: the apostles, the prophets, the evangelists, and the pastors and teachers" (Ephesians 4:11).

- *Preach the Good News*—"And then he told them, 'Go into all the world and preach the Good News to everyone, everywhere'" (Mark 16:15).

- *Tell them*—"Go home to your friends, and tell them what wonderful things the Lord has done for you and how merciful he has been" (Mark 5:19).

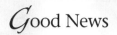

## *G*ood News

In the Bible, the Good News and the Gospel are the same thing. They both describe the way of salvation in Jesus. That's why you'll sometimes hear people talk about "spreading the Good News" or "preaching the Gospel."

- *Let your light shine*—"Don't hide your light under a basket! Instead, put it on a stand and let it shine for all" (Matthew 5:15).

- *Show others*—"This is so you can show others the goodness of God, for he called you out of the darkness into his wonderful light" (1 Peter 2:9).

- *Plant seeds*—"My job was to plant the seed in your hearts, and Apollos watered it, but it was God, not we, who made it grow" (1 Corinthians 3:6).

### Don't Try to Convince

If you were to look up all of these words and phrases in *Strong's Concordance* (a very useful book) you would find something very interesting. All of them involve declaring, proclaiming, reporting, showing, scattering, speaking, and publishing the Good News about Jesus Christ and what He has done for us. In other words, sharing your faith!

The problem is that many of us think sharing our faith involves convincing, convicting, and converting. No wonder we're afraid! Who wants to take on that kind of responsibility? Well, you can relax because God doesn't expect us to do any of that. We couldn't convince, convict, and convert anyone even if we tried. Only God can do these things.

- The love of God through Christ *convinces* us (Romans 8:38).

- The work of God through the Holy Spirit *convicts* us (John 16:8 NIV).

- The grace of God through our faith *converts* us (1 Corinthians 3:7).

### Just Act Naturally

Sharing your faith should be the most natural thing in the world because it's really nothing more than telling someone else the story of what God has done for you. When you talk about Jesus with one other person, you are sharing your faith. When you tell the story of your spiritual journey in front of a group (even if your knees are knocking), you are sharing your faith. When you tell people about Jesus in a letter or an e-mail—or you give them a book about Jesus—you are sharing your faith.

The reason many of us are reluctant to share our faith is that we worry about what other people will say or do. We're afraid they might say no. We think we might be ridiculed. We are concerned that we might offend someone. Don't worry about it! Sharing your faith isn't about you. Sharing your faith isn't even about the other person saying yes, no, or maybe. It's all about God and His incredible gift to us. All He wants us to do is share the gift. He promises to do the rest.

## Why Doesn't God Do It Himself?

You might be wondering, *Hey, if salvation is so important* (and it is), *why doesn't God tell everyone Himself?* Well, He has—in at least four different ways that we can think of:

1. God has placed the truth about Himself in the *heart* of every human being (Romans 1:19).

2. God has placed the truth about Himself in *nature* (Romans 1:20).

3. God has placed the truth about Himself in the *Bible* (2 Timothy 3:15-16).

4. God has placed the truth about Himself in *Jesus* (John 10:30; 14:9).

Isn't it reassuring to know that God doesn't expect you to tell others about Him without backup? When you share your faith, you don't have to trudge through unknown territory. God has already made a way.

## The Method to God's Plan

There are some very good reasons why God wants us to share our faith. These reasons have to do with our ultimate purpose, God's ultimate plan, and God's chosen path.

### Our Ultimate Purpose

Do you ever wonder why you exist in the first place? You should! It's the number one question people have asked through the ages. And here's the number one answer:

> *For everything comes from him; everything exists by his power and is intended for his glory. To him be glory evermore. Amen* (Romans 11:36).

There you have it. You exist in order to glorify God. That's why God created you. And when you talk to others about God, you glorify Him whether they respond or not.

### God's Ultimate Plan

God isn't some old gray-haired man sitting on a cloud in heaven, waiting to zap us when we do wrong. Neither is He a big benign celestial Santa Claus who only looks at the good stuff we do. God is the holy, dynamic, personal, loving Creator of the universe. He made us to glorify Him and to enjoy Him. But He can't relate to us as long as our lives are characterized by sin. So God made a way for us to come back to Him through Jesus. This is His ultimate plan.

> *His unchanging plan has always been to adopt us into his own family by bringing us to himself through Jesus Christ. And this gave him great pleasure* (Ephesians 1:5).

This is what God wants you to share with others. The essence of your faith is Jesus, and when you share it, God is pleased.

### God's Chosen Path

See how this works? God created us to glorify Him, but sin cut us off from God. So God revealed His plan, which was to bring us back to Him through the death and resurrection of His Son,

Jesus. That's the gift of salvation. When we receive the gift by faith, we automatically become a part of all believers everywhere, collectively known as the church. As a member of this universal church (also known as the body of Christ), we have an obligation:

- to worship God (Ephesians 5:16-19)

- to serve one another (1 Peter 4:8-11)

- to share our faith (Mark 16:15)

---

$\mathcal{B}$elievers need...three vital experiences to grow into mature Christians. They need good Bible teaching that will give them theological and spiritual stability; they need deep and satisfying relationships both with each other and with Jesus Christ; and they need to experience seeing people come to Jesus Christ as a result of corporate and individual witness to the non-Christian world.

*Gene Getz*

---

## The Great Commission

We hope you are beginning to realize that sharing your faith is not optional for the believer. It's not just for pastors, missionaries, Sunday school teachers, or TV evangelists. If you have received Jesus as your personal Savior, then telling others about your faith is your responsibility and privilege.

If you need more convincing, all you have to do is read some of the last words Jesus spoke while on earth. All four of Jesus' biographers wrote down these words, which have become known as the Great Commission:

- Matthew recorded the best-known statement of the Great Commission, where the emphasis is on the authority of Christ (Matthew 28:18-20).

- Mark was very clear that anyone who rejects the Good News will be condemned (Mark 16:15-16).

- Luke reminds us that Jesus fulfilled prophecy by coming to earth and dying for our sins (Luke 24:46-47).

- John wrote that Jesus was commissioned to be a light to the world, and so are we (John 20:21).

- Finally, in the book of Acts (also written by Luke) we learn that the Great Commission is no empty command. Jesus has given us the power to share our faith:

*When the Holy Spirit has come upon you, you will receive power and will tell people about me everywhere—in Jerusalem, throughout Judea, in Samaria, and to the ends of the earth* (Acts 1:8).

By the way, notice that Jesus' words are not called the Great Suggestion or the Great Idea. This is a *commission*, which is defined as a "written order giving certain powers, privileges, and duties." That's exactly what Jesus has laid out for us. Make no mistake about it. *Sharing your faith is not optional.*

## Be Among the 5 Percent

Greg Laurie, a pastor and evangelist, says that "95 percent of all Christians have never led another person to Christ." That's a sad and sobering statistic, because it probably means that 95 percent of all Christians aren't actively sharing their faith. What this also means is that 95 percent of all Christians aren't paying attention to the Great Commission. Do you want to be in the 95 percent, or do you want to be among the 5 percent who share their faith and lead people to Christ? The choice is yours!

### Having the Heart of Jesus

Our salvation is based on the person and work of Jesus, "on whom our faith depends from start to finish" (Hebrews 12:2). Doesn't it make sense that we should not only follow Jesus but also imitate Him in all we do?

There's no question about it. We need to live like Jesus would live. We need to have the heart of Jesus, which came out in the life He lived here on earth. When you study the life of Christ in the Bible, here's what you find:

- Jesus came to earth to save us, not condemn us (John 3:17). We are already dead in our sins, but God offers the free gift of eternal life through Jesus (Romans 6:23).

- Jesus doesn't want anyone to die in his or her sins. He wants as many people to be saved as possible. In fact, He is delaying His return so that more people will be saved (2 Peter 3:9).

- Jesus is praying for everyone who will eventually believe in Him (John 17:20).

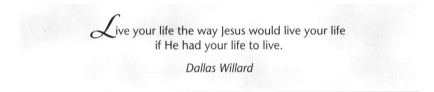

*Live your life the way Jesus would live your life if He had your life to live.*

*Dallas Willard*

The heart of Jesus breaks for the lost. He died for all people, but only those who believe in Him can have eternal life (John 3:16). Just like Jesus, we need hearts that break for people without Christ. We need to see people without Christ—whether they are our friends, neighbors, coworkers, family members, or complete strangers—as people without hope. They have a fatal disease called sin, and the only cure is Christ. We know that, and we need to tell them.

The first place to start as you prepare to share your faith is to pray for the lost. This is critical! If you want to have the heart of Jesus, you need to pray for the people Jesus died for.

> *I urge you, first of all, to pray for all people. As you make your requests, plead for God's mercy upon them, and give thanks.... This is good and pleases God our Savior, for he wants everyone to be saved and to understand the truth* (1 Timothy 2:1,3-4).

### Salvation Is for Everyone

Christ can save anyone. God loves every person who has ever lived, and He has made His salvation available to anyone who asks (Romans 10:13). But there's a catch, a condition. Others won't know unless we tell them! Unless we share our faith, they won't believe. It's as simple and as serious as that.

> *But how can they call on him to save them unless they believe in him? And how can they believe in him if they have never heard about him? And how can they hear about him unless someone tells them? And how will anyone go and tell them without being sent? That is what the Scriptures mean when they say, "How beautiful are the feet of those who bring good news!"* (Romans 10:14-15).

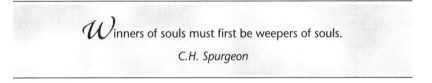

*W*inners of souls must first be weepers of souls.

C.H. Spurgeon

## You've Got all the Help You Need

The responsibility to share your faith with others, to have the heart of Jesus, and to pray for the lost may seem a little overwhelming. It should! This is serious business. That's why God has given every Christian two supernatural resources to help us do what He wants us to do: The Word of God and the Holy Spirit.

### The Word of God

God is available to teach you through His personal training manual, the Bible. More than an ordinary book, the Bible contains the very words of God. The Bible is God's living message for you. It contains everything you need to live and grow as a Christian (2 Timothy 3:16-17). As you read the Bible daily, here are three things you should do:

- *Study*—make an effort to systematically learn God's Word (2 Timothy 2:15).

- *Meditate*—think deeply about God's Word (Psalm 1:2).

- *Memorize*—be ready to recall God's Word (Psalm 119:11).

Not only will you please God when you read His message to you, but you will learn at least three important components to your witnessing efforts:

- how to live and grow as a Christian (1 Peter 2:2)

- how to develop spiritual discernment (Acts 17:11)

- how to answer the questions of others (1 Peter 3:15)

### The Holy Spirit

Trying to share your faith without the Bible is futile. Sharing your faith without the Holy Spirit is foolish. This is because the Holy Spirit gives you power in at least three different ways. Without this power, the life you live and the words you say will fall totally flat.

- *The Holy Spirit guides you.* As a Christian, you have a tremendous advantage over the person who doesn't know God personally. You have the Holy Spirit in your life (1 Corinthians 12:13), and one of His primary functions is to "guide you into all truth" (John 16:13). This isn't your average, everyday truth. This is truth about God and His ways. There is no greater truth!

  *But we know these things because God has revealed them to us by his Spirit, and his Spirit searches out everything and shows us even God's deep secrets* (1 Corinthians 2:10).

- *The Holy Spirit enlightens others.* The reason it's foolish to share your faith without the Holy Spirit is that the message of the Gospel is foolish to anyone who doesn't know God personally (1 Corinthians 2:14). Do you ever wonder why nonbelievers often shake their heads when they hear Christians talk about God? It's because their minds are literally blinded to the things of God. Unless the

Holy Spirit opens their hearts and their minds to receive our message, nothing will happen. Here's what the apostle Paul wrote about preaching to the church at Corinth:

> *I came to you in weakness—timid and trembling. And my message and my preaching were very plain. I did not use wise and persuasive speeches, but the Holy Spirit was powerful among you. I did this so that you might trust the power of God rather than human wisdom* (1 Corinthians 2:3-5).

It's the power of the Holy Spirit—and not merely your words—that will ultimately lead someone to receive the message of the Gospel. Remember, your job is to *proclaim* the Good News. It's up to the Holy Spirit to *convict* and *convince*.

---

*W*hen you're witnessing to someone, you have to allow the Spirit of God to do His work. When you do that, you'll be encouraged and rewarded to know that the Holy Spirit will use you in the lives of those who don't know Christ.

*John MacArthur*

---

- *The Holy Spirit prays when you don't know what to pray for.* Paul, in his letter to the church in Rome, states another incredible benefit of having the Holy Spirit in your life:

> *And the Holy Spirit helps us in our distress. For we don't even know what we should pray for, nor how we should pray. But the Holy Spirit prays for us with groanings that cannot be expressed in words. And the Father who knows all hearts knows what the Spirit is saying, for the Spirit pleads for us believers in harmony with God's own will* (Romans 8:26-27).

Think about that for a minute. When you don't know how to pray or what to pray for, the Holy Spirit prays on your behalf in ways you can't even imagine. Is your heart burdened for an unsaved friend, yet you don't know what to say or how to pray? The Holy Spirit is way ahead of you. He is already praying to the Father for you and your friend.

## Know What You Believe

When you first accept Jesus as your Savior, you're a little like the blind man Jesus healed. When he was asked to talk about Jesus, the man said he didn't know a lot about Him. "But I know this: I was blind, and now I can see!" (John 9:25). In the same way, as a new believer you can testify to the dramatic change in your life, and this can be a powerful witness. But as you "learn to know God better and better" (Colossians 1:10), your faith will grow because you will know more about Jesus and your Christian life. This will give you greater confidence as you share your faith with others because you will know the "why" and the "what" of your Christian faith. In other words, *why* people need to turn to Jesus for salvation and *what* is involved.

Growing as a Christian involves more than simply gaining knowledge about God, but you will never grow without that knowledge. And you will have a hard time answering the questions people have about your faith. That's why you need to have a working knowledge of the basics of your Christian life. The following list doesn't cover everything you need to know, but it's a pretty good start.

*1. The Bible*

The Bible is God's inspired, inerrant message to us. The Bible gives us direction (Psalm 119:105), shows us right and wrong (Psalm 119:11), and shows us the truth about ourselves (Hebrews 4:12).

*2. God*

God is the self-existent, infinite, holy, personal Creator of the universe. God has always existed, and He created the universe by the power of His Word (Hebrews 11:3). There is only one true God (Isaiah 45:5). In the unity of the Godhead there are three persons of one substance—the Father, the Son, and the Holy Spirit—with distinct personalities.

### 3. Jesus Christ

Jesus is the only begotten Son of God, yet completely God and one with the Father (John 10:30). Jesus is the Mediator between God and humankind, having been sent by God to earth to die for us and to forgive our sins (John 1:29).

### 4. The Death and Resurrection of Jesus

Jesus died on the cross, was buried, and after three days rose from the dead (1 Corinthians 15:3-4). After 40 days Jesus ascended into heaven, where He is at the right hand of the Father (Hebrews 1:3), pleading to God on our behalf (1 John 2:1).

### 5. Man and Sin

God created humans in His image (Genesis 1:26-27) with an eternal soul (Matthew 10:28). Our chief end is to glorify God and enjoy Him forever. Yet the entire human race falls short of God's perfect standard because of sin (Romans 3:23). Our sin leads to death, but God has given us eternal life through Jesus Christ (Romans 6:23).

### 6. Salvation

We are saved from our sins and death by believing in the person and work of Jesus Christ (John 3:16). We can do nothing to earn our salvation; it is God's gracious gift to us (Ephesians 2:8-9). Once you believe by faith that God has saved you by His grace in Jesus, you are secure in Christ for eternity (John 10:28-29).

### 7. The Holy Spirit

The Holy Spirit, the third person of the Godhead, has always existed with God the Father and Jesus Christ. The Holy Spirit baptizes every believer into the body of Christ (1 Corinthians 12:13) and gives each of us spiritual gifts and empowers us to bear spiritual fruit when we give Him control of our lives (Galatians 5:22-23). The Holy Spirit is our guarantee that Jesus Christ is coming back for His church (2 Corinthians 1:21-22).

## 8. *Angels, Satan, and Demons*

The spirit world is very real. It is made up of God's messengers, called angels, and God's enemies, Satan and his demons (Ephesians 6:12). Satan is also the enemy of the believer (1 Peter 5:8), and he blinds the mind of the unbeliever (2 Corinthians 4:4). Satan and his allies are ultimately doomed to defeat (Revelation 20:10).

## 9. *The Church*

The church is the universal body of Christ, comprised of all believers everywhere. The church exists so that we can worship God (Ephesians 5:16-19), serve one another (Ephesians 4:12), and share our faith (Mark 16:15).

## 10. *Future Things*

God has a plan for the future, which includes the end of the world as we know it and the creation of a new heaven and a new earth. The focal point of God's future plan is the second coming of Christ, which will happen unexpectedly (Matthew 24:44). Judgment and eternal life in hell await the unbeliever (Revelation 20:15). All those who have believed in Jesus Christ will spend eternity in heaven, which Jesus is preparing for us (John 14:1-3).

Once again we want to emphasize that mere knowledge about God won't save you. Remember, salvation is a gift of God that you receive by faith. But your knowledge of God and what He has done for you will give you confidence as you live your Christian life and share it with others.

# How to Share
# the Gift of Salvation

When you begin to actively share your faith with others, you will have many opportunities to explain God's plan of salvation, and you will know when someone is ready to meet God personally. Here are six steps to knowing God that you can share when the time is right:

> *Step 1*—God loves you and wants to have a relationship with you (John 3:16).

> *Step 2*—You will never satisfy God's perfect standards (Romans 3:23).

> *Step 3*—Jesus did something you could never do: He died for your sins (Romans 5:8).

> *Step 4*—The only way to God is through Jesus (John 14:6).

> *Step 5*—Jesus is knocking at the door of your heart (Revelation 3:20).

> *Step 6*—You need to personally receive Jesus Christ into your life (Romans 10:9).

You may want to write these steps on a blank page in your Bible. Better yet, memorize the steps and the Bible verses so you can respond any time to someone who wants to connect with God personally.

# What's That Again?

1. Salvation is the greatest gift in the world, and it's a gift that's meant to be shared, not kept as a secret.

2. The Bible describes sharing your faith in many different ways, and they all involve declaring, proclaiming, showing, scattering, and speaking the Good News about Jesus Christ. Nowhere are we told to convince, convict, or convert others.

3. We should be sharing our faith for at least three reasons: 1) It fulfills our ultimate purpose, which is to glorify God; 2) when we share our faith, God is pleased; and 3) sharing our faith helps others discover the path to salvation and membership in God's universal church.

4. The Great Commission is our written order, given by Jesus, to tell others about Him. Sharing your faith is not optional.

5. We need to have the heart of Jesus, whose heart broke for the lost. This begins by praying for people to be saved.

6. God has given you two supernatural resources to help you share your faith: the Bible and the Holy Spirit.

7. In order to grow as a Christian, you need to know what you believe. You need to have a working knowledge of the basics of your Christian faith.

## Dig Deeper

Here are some of our favorite books about sharing and better understanding your faith.

> *How to Share Your Faith* by Greg Laurie, the pastor of a huge church that has grown primarily through people sharing their faith.
>
> *Nothing but the Truth* by John MacArthur. What should you say when asked about your faith? This book provides solid, biblical answers.
>
> *The Master Plan of Discipleship* by Robert E. Coleman shows how the disciples fulfilled the Great Commission and how we can do the same today.
>
> *Know What You Believe* by Paul Little. This classic book explains the fundamentals of the Christian faith.
>
> *Knowing God 101* by Bruce Bickel and Stan Jantz gives you the basics of your faith in our typical style (correct, clear, and casual).

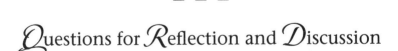

# *Q*uestions for *R*eflection and *D*iscussion

1. What is the greatest gift (besides salvation) you ever received? Describe what happened after you got the gift.

2. What is salvation and why do we need it? Why is it sometimes difficult to explain salvation to someone who doesn't think they need to be saved?

3. When it comes to being a witness for Christ, why does the Lord expect us to share our faith rather than try to convince others they need to be saved? Why do we continue to put

pressure on ourselves by thinking we have to convince others?

4. Describe how God has placed the truth about Himself in—

   • the heart of every person

   • nature

   • the Bible

   • Jesus

5. Look up the five Scripture references for the Great Commission (in the four Gospels and in Acts). What is common to all of these verses? What is unique to each one?

6. What does it mean to have a broken heart for the lost? How should this change your approach to someone who is without hope, whether it's a spouse, a friend, or a neighbor? Should you be more compassionate or more direct in your witnessing efforts?

7. Describe a time when the Holy Spirit helped you relate to someone else. How often does this happen to you? What can you do to experience more of this kind of divine intervention?

8. What practical things are you doing to grow in your knowledge of God?

## Moving On...

This chapter has covered the "nuts and bolts" of your faith and how you share it. Now it's time to look at the basics of your life and how you live it, because what you do speaks louder than what you say.

# *C*hapter 8

Preach the Gospel at all times. When
necessary, use words.

*St. Francis of Assisi*

When people think about witnessing, they usually worry about the words they are going to say. The words you speak about Jesus are important. Words are used to *explain* how a person can establish a personal relationship with Jesus. Words can also be used to *describe* how Jesus transformed your life from the inside out, but words aren't the only method you have for witnessing.

Don't think about witnessing only in terms of what you say. In many ways your behavior—your lifestyle—is the most effective way to show people how God has changed your life. All of your words about the love of God will be useless if your lifestyle fails to reflect God's love. On the other hand, when your life is a reflection of the love of God, people will notice that your life is different, and they'll want you to tell them why. When you witness to others through your actions, your words take on meaning.

In this chapter, we're going to talk about the importance of lining up your *walk* with your *talk*. Then we'll outline some ways you can answer the questions people ask you because they know your life is different.

# How to Share
# Your Faith

*I*n the last chapter, we focused on sharing your faith in the context of what you should *say* to someone about God. And isn't that what you have been worrying about all along—what *words* to use and when to say them? Well, now that we've covered that area, we have some good news (and bad news) for you:

*The good news:* We have told you all you need to know for sharing with someone the basics of being a Christian. You can stop worrying. You've got all the necessary words.

*The bad news:* The words aren't the hardest part of sharing your faith. In fact, they may be the easiest part. The truth is that *living* your faith is much harder than *explaining* it.

## People You Know and People You Don't

We don't mean to oversimplify things, but there are two kinds of people in the world: People you know and people you don't. Throughout your life, you will have the opportunity to share your faith with both groups.

### People You Don't Know

These are the people that you will only see once and then probably never again. This group includes

- the lady waiting next to you at the airport,

- the guy standing ahead of you in the "12 items or less" line at the supermarket, and

- the gas station attendant who gives you directions when you are lost.

Of course, you should be ready to share your faith with these people, but often the circumstances don't seem just right for doing so.

- The lady at the airport heard you lose your temper at the counter when your flight was delayed. She saw you make the ticket agent cry. She cowers whenever you move toward her, so you probably won't be able to get close enough to talk with her about the inner peace that comes from knowing Jesus.

- You yelled at the guy in the grocery line because you counted the items in his cart, and he had 13 of them. Of course, he qualified to stay in the line after he threw a package of frozen peas at you.

- You're too rushed to talk to the gas station attendant. You have to make up for all that time you spent driving around before you worked up the nerve to ask someone for directions.

We aren't saying that you shouldn't try to share your faith with strangers. You should. And, if your conduct in that brief contact with them doesn't immediately ruin your credibility, the words you speak might answer one of their spiritual questions. Your reference to a personal relationship with God in that casual conversation might be the encouragement they need to start seeking God. Encounters with people you don't know happen every day, in all sorts of circumstances, and you never know when you'll have an opportunity to share your faith. But we think that sharing your faith will happen more often and more effectively with the other group of people.

### People You Know

These are the people who see you all of the time. You keep running into them because they are in your network of relationships. This group includes:

- *The members of your family.* This group is difficult to avoid because you share a refrigerator and a bathroom with them.

- *Your relatives and in-laws.* You see them only a few times a year, but sometimes that is more than enough. Even if they only come at Thanksgiving, you remember them all year long (because they left that cranberry sauce stain on the dining room carpet).

- *The people you go to school with or know from work.* Some of them may be your friends—others may be your enemies—but you see them almost every day.

- *The people in your neighborhood.* You may know some better than others, but your residential proximity means that you see them on a fairly regular basis.

These are the people you are most likely to share your faith with. Why? Because you have the most contact with them. Actually, your continuing relationships are one of those "good news, bad news" situations. Here we go again:

*The good news:* You see the people you know on a frequent basis. You will have lots of opportunities to share your faith with them.

*The bad news:* They see you all of the time. They know what kind of a person you are. They might not think much of what you say about Christianity if they don't think much of you.

With people who know you, the words you speak are not the only way that you share your faith about God. Before you even get the words out of your mouth, these people have already had an opportunity to observe your lifestyle. Their opinion of you—based on what they have observed—will influence them more than any words that you can say.

## You Are a Witness

"Witnessing" doesn't just happen when you are explaining John 3:16 to someone. It happens all of the time, every moment of your life. If you are a Christian, you are a witness 24 hours a day, seven days a week. During those hours, people are watching your reactions (okay, except during the hours when you are sleeping). The people you know see you almost every day. If they know you are a Christian, they are likely to evaluate Christianity based on your conduct.

### Whether You Want to Be or Not

Notice that this witness thing happens whether you want it to or not. Oh sure, we all want our unsaved family and friends to be paying attention to us when we go to church or volunteer at the Rescue Mission. In other words, we don't mind them scrutinizing our behavior when we are acting spiritual. But we sure don't want them noticing what we do and say when

- we yell a few "unpleasantries" at the referee who made a bad call at our kid's soccer game,
- we're laughing at a crude and offensive joke, or
- a driver cuts us off on the freeway, and we mutter something about his intelligence or his upbringing.

These are just a few examples. We each have our own special set of sins we would be ashamed for people to see.

### Act like Christ Before You Talk About Christ

Effective witnessing involves a combination of your character, your conduct, and your communication. All of these aspects of your life should be reflections of Jesus Christ. That is what witnessing is all about—telling and showing other people what Jesus is like. You can *tell* them by what you *say*, but you *show* them by what you *do*.

---

*W*hat you do speaks so loud that I can't hear what you say.

*Anonymous*

---

## Become More Like Christ

As Christians, we should be engaged in the ongoing effort to become more like Christ in our thoughts, deeds, and words. That is what is involved in sharing our faith. When we do whatever is necessary to be a fully devoted follower of Christ, we are doing everything necessary for witnessing. This process involves

- pursuing the character of Christ,
- practicing the deeds of Christ, and
- presenting the simplicity of Christ.

### Pursue the Character of Christ

In his usual blunt fashion, the apostle Paul laid it on the line:

*Your attitude should be the same that Christ Jesus had* (Philippians 2:5).

If you want to have the attitude and character of Christ, you have to change your whole way of thinking. You can't trust your natural instincts because they are the opposite of God's spiritual instincts. You can have a Christlike attitude only after God has been able to transform your thinking.

*Let God transform you into a new person by changing the way you think. Then you will know what God wants you to do* (Romans 12:2).

Being like Christ sounds impossible. Actually, it is if we try to do it by ourselves. But God, through the Holy Spirit, gives us the ability to be like Christ.

*And as the Spirit of the Lord works within us, we become more and more like him and reflect his glory even more* (2 Corinthians 3:18).

As we give God more control of our lives, we will start to exhibit His character in our lives. The traits of Christ, as listed in Galatians 5:22-23, will start to pop up. In a world filled with anger, selfishness, and hostility, people will start to notice something different about us when we exhibit love, joy, peace, patience, kindness, goodness, faithfulness, gentleness, and self-control.

# How to Prove You Are a Follower of Christ

Jesus explained the way that we can become credible witnesses for Him and prove to the world that we are His followers. Interestingly, it isn't by declaring our allegiance to Him by any oath. The proof comes not from words but from our love for each other.

*Your love for one another will prove to the world that you are my disciples* (John 13:35).

### Practice the Deeds of Christ

Do you remember the WWJD phenomenon? Maybe you still have a WWJD bracelet left in your desk drawer (or maybe it's still on your wrist). "What Would Jesus Do?" was not a gimmick invented by some clever marketers. Jesus is the One who started it when He said,

*I have given you an example to follow. Do as I have done to you* (John 13:15).

Don't worry about trying to copy everything Jesus did. You don't have to start with walking on water or turning water into wine. Your unsaved family and friends might be more impressed if you simply

- don't retaliate when someone is rude to you,

- make (or at least buy) a dinner for your neighbors when they are sick,

- treat homeless people with dignity,

- take time out of your busy schedule to help a friend move, or

- give your seat on the commuter train to someone else.

The best way to *explain* the love of Christ is to be an *example* of the love of Christ.

## Don't Worry If You Aren't Perfect

No one expects you to be perfect. Not even your in-laws. It will be enough if you are making an honest attempt to be Christlike in your character and conduct. After all, part of telling people about God is the admission that none of us is perfect. D.T. Niles said it this way: "Christianity is one beggar telling another beggar where to find food."

### Present the Simplicity of Christ

If you have been modeling the character and conduct of Christ, you will have established the credibility to talk about your faith with your family and friends who don't know about Him. In fact, they might be anxious to know what makes you so different from other people. As you explain what Jesus has done in your life, remember to keep it simple: Just tell them about Jesus.

Jesus said that we are supposed to be His witnesses (Acts 1:8). That means we just tell people what we know about Him. Plain and simple.

- *We aren't supposed to be Jesus' public relations agent.* He doesn't need us to build up a bunch of hype about Him. Don't alter what you have to say based on what you think your friends want to hear. Just tell them about Jesus as you know Him.

- *We aren't His sales force.* We aren't paid on a commission based on how many people we get to sign a "salvation" contract. We shouldn't use pressure tactics.

- *He doesn't need a marketing strategist.* Don't think that you need to trick people into learning about Jesus. Be upfront and straightforward with people. Jesus can take it from there.

People don't need a religion, but they do need Jesus. Don't get distracted from this simple message: Jesus loves them, He died on the cross to pay the penalty for their sins, and He wants to establish a personal relationship with them.

### Loving Works Better than Lecturing

Leave the sermons to the pastors. Your friends and family don't want to hear any preaching from you. They don't need to be lectured, scolded, or ridiculed. You are not properly representing Jesus if you are alienating these people when you present the Gospel message to them. Sure, they are sinners, but so are you. Jesus hates your sin, but He loves you. And you should show that same love to all of the unsaved people you know. Sharing your faith effectively—through your character, your conduct, and your words—is simply the natural outgrowth of loving God.

- As you love God more, you will be more excited about the things He is doing in your life. Your excitement about

God will make it easier for you to talk to other people about Him.

- As you love God more, your understanding of Him will grow. Your relationship with Him will become even more personal. It will be easier for you to explain your relationship with God to those who don't know Him.

- As you love God more, you won't have to force yourself to share your faith. You will be doing it naturally—your deeds and words will be a testimony of God's love—because the Holy Spirit is producing God's character in your life.

- As you love God more, you will begin to feel His love for the unsaved. You will be looking for opportunities to share God's love to family, friends, and strangers who are spiritually lost.

## The Great Thing About Skeptics

Once again, at the risk of oversimplifying, there are two kinds of unsaved people in the world:

- *Seekers:* These are people who are already "God-sensitive." They know there is a spiritual dimension to life, and they are looking for answers. Seekers are easy to talk to about God because they want to hear what you have to say. They are usually more anxious to listen than you are to talk.

- *Skeptics:* These are tough nuts to crack. They are so hard to convince. Many times they don't even want to get into a discussion about spiritual matters.

Now, you might think that hanging out with the seekers and avoiding the skeptics would be a more effective use of your time. It is natural to think that way because it would make your witnessing easier. But don't shun the skeptics. For the most part they are simply seekers with tough questions. Once you understand this, you won't be so intimidated. Besides, there are some really great reasons why you need to share your faith with them:

*1. Jesus loves the skeptic as much as He loves the seeker.* Somebody needs to talk with them about Him.

*2. Talking with skeptics can actually strengthen your faith.* They may force you to deal with issues and questions about Jesus and Christianity that you ignored or glossed over in your own personal spiritual journey. Don't be afraid to explore these issues. They won't shake your faith because you already know the truth. And you've got the Holy Spirit on your side to help you come to the correct conclusion on these tough issues.

> *He [the Holy Spirit] will guide you into all truth* (John 16:13).

*3. Skeptics have strong feelings and opinions about Jesus.* That's good, even though their attitude toward Christ is a negative one. Their intensity against spiritual matters makes them good candidates to receive the Gospel. They will want to challenge what you say and believe about Christ. If they approach the challenge with intellectual integrity, they will have to look at the evidence about Christ and consider all that He said and did. God has promised that those who honestly look for Him will find Him.

> *"If you look for me in earnest, you will find me when you seek me. I will be found by you," says the* Lord (Jeremiah 29:13-14).

*4. As you interact with skeptics, you will gain confidence in your ability to share your faith.* You'll begin to realize that the Holy Spirit guides your thoughts and your responses. You'll recognize that most of the objections fall into a few basic categories that can be easily answered (see the following section).

In your own network of friends, skeptics are not likely to be hostile toward you (or toward Christianity) if you have been living a life that reflects the love of Jesus. Oh, they still might argue with your viewpoints, but they'll respect the sincerity of your beliefs because you have the lifestyle that gives your faith credibility. And that is what witnessing is all about—establishing a rapport with people and earning their respect so that you have the opportunity to be heard.

# Some Really Famous Christians Started Out as Skeptics

Skeptics who become Christians usually have a very strong faith because they really tested the claims of Christianity before they made their decision.

- One of the very first skeptics was Saul, who later was known as the apostle Paul. He was persecuting and killing Christians before he had his encounter with Christ. You can't get much more skeptical than that.

- C.S. Lewis is a renowned theologian. His books, including *The Screwtape Letters* and the Chronicles of Narnia series, are Christian classics. C.S. Lewis was a skeptic who tried to disprove the existence of God. Guess what happened?

- *Evidence That Demands a Verdict* is one of our favorite books for looking at the logical reasons to believe in Jesus. The author, Josh McDowell, knows a lot about the objections of skeptics, because he used to be one.

## Questions and Objections You'll Love to Answer

As you spend time talking to skeptics about their problems with Christianity, we think you'll discover an interesting phenomenon: Their objections and questions fall into a few basic categories. Skeptics may articulate their disbelief in different ways, but most of the time these are all variations on the same basic issues. Here are seven of the most common ones:

*1. The skeptics ask, "Can you prove that God exists?"* The pat answer is "Well, you can't prove that He doesn't exist." That's true, but resist pat answers because skeptics aren't persuaded by them (and you don't want to reduce the discussion to a level of sarcasm). Remember that you are talking to a skeptic who has been raised in a postmodern society that believes that truth is relative. With that kind of a philosophical background, the question is an honest one.

Don't let this question shake you. Just look around. The cosmos at large, and the human body and mind in particular, are ample proof that an intelligent designer is at work in the universe. If your skeptic is a fan of Darwin and says that all that exists is the result of a few random molecules colliding together by chance, then we suggest that you both read a book like *Darwin on Trial* by Phillip Johnson that examines the question of God's existence from a scientific approach. (Tell your skeptic friend that Phillip Johnson is a professor from U.C. Berkeley. It's true, and most skeptics love Berkeley professors.)

*2. The skeptics ask, "How can a loving God allow evil and suffering in the world?"* This does sound sort of incongruous, doesn't it? Look at the inconsistencies from the skeptic's point of view:

- Tragic things happen to innocent people. (Babies are born with deformities, children are dying of starvation, and around the world people are suffering under the rule of oppressive governments.)

- And just as contradictory, good things happen to bad people. (In our own country, murderers escape justice, and on the international scene, tyrants live in luxury.)

- To someone who lacks a biblical perspective of the world, it would seem that either God doesn't care or He is powerless to do anything about it.

You should compliment the skeptic for asking such an insightful question. Let's be honest that some things do seem unfair. As Christians we know that God is pure love, so we can trust

His judgment in these circumstances. But the skeptic doesn't trust God (yet), so what is a reasonable response?

The Bible says that evil exists in the world because mankind has chosen to rebel against God. Every human is infected with a sin virus. That is where evil finds its source. In some people, the evil is contained in large part; in others, the evil is expressed without restrictions. If God were to eliminate all of the evil from the world, He would obliterate humanity off the face of the earth. But God has not ignored the condition of wickedness and anguish in the world. Through Jesus Christ, God has provided a way for us to have eternal life in heaven with no evil or suffering. In the perspective of eternity, our life on earth is only momentary. Through a relationship with Christ, we can be assured of an eternal life in heaven. And while we are stuck here on earth, God gives us spiritual strength and perspective to deal with the tough times in life.

> *Don't worry about anything; instead, pray about everything. Tell God what you need, and thank him for all he has done. If you do this, you will experience God's peace, which is far more wonderful than the human mind can understand. His peace will guard your hearts and minds as you live in Christ Jesus* (Philippians 4:6-7).

*3. The skeptics ask, "How can a loving God send people to hell?"* This question can be easily answered when you realize that its premise is incorrect. God does not send people to hell. Hell is what they deserve because of their sin. They are going to hell on their own. But because God is loving, He has provided a way to rescue them.

*4. The skeptics ask: "What about people who have never heard about Jesus?"* This is a question that doesn't occur only to skeptics. A lot of Christians wonder about this issue. Since Christ's death on the cross 2000 years ago, millions of people have lived and died without hearing the Gospel message. And even in our own generation of satellite television broadcasts, remote villages in less developed countries don't have the luxury of electricity or missionaries. So what happens to all of those people who die without having a chance to make a decision about God?

If you are looking to us for the definitive answer, you are going to be disappointed. We don't have just one, complete, authoritative answer. But we have several partial answers. First, we know that God is just and fair. Because we can have confidence in His attributes (His character traits), we can be assured that no one is being treated unfairly. Secondly, the Bible says that nature provides enough evidence to make God's existence obvious to anyone. (Check out Romans 1:19-20 and Psalm 19.)

The fact that we can't provide a satisfactory answer for this question isn't a legitimate excuse for rejecting Christ. (The Bible says that some aspects of God are kept secret from mankind. See Deuteronomy 29:29.) At the end of the world, when the skeptics stand before Jesus at the time of judgment, there will be no "Get Out of Hell Free" cards issued to them. The only relevant question at that time will be how they responded to Jesus, not how God handled the people in remote villages.

5. *The skeptics ask, "How can the Bible be trusted when it has so many inconsistencies?"* You can have a lot of fun with this one, but go easy. Ask your skeptic friends for an example of the inconsistencies that are bothering them. Usually, people don't know of any inconsistencies; they have just heard that as a common criticism, so they are repeating it. The reliability of the Bible has been challenged over the centuries. If there were any evidence that truly discredited the Bible, it would be highly publicized. Actually, the contrary is true. All recent archaeological discoveries have proven that the Bible is accurate and reliable from a historical point of view. If your skeptic has legitimate, sincere questions about the content of the Bible, they probably can be explained by a better understanding of the Bible:

- *How it was written.* The Holy Spirit inspired the various authors. So they wrote God's message, but they did it in their own vernacular and from their own perspectives. For example, there are differences in the four New Testament biographies about Jesus (Matthew, Mark, Luke, and

John). The differences have nothing to do with errors or inconsistencies. It's just that the authors had such differences in backgrounds. (You can't get much more diverse than a tax collector, a physician, and a fisherman.)

- *How it was transcribed.* There is an interesting history about how God's Word has been preserved and passed from the ancient scrolls. Scholars of ancient literature acknowledge the accuracy in the transcription of the various manuscripts.

- *How it has been translated.* Different translations don't make the Bible unreliable. As culture changes, so does the language. Contemporary translations rely on the ancient manuscripts and the most current linguistics.

*6. The skeptics object, "Christianity is too intolerant."* By this objection, the skeptics are usually referring to the fact that Christ claimed to be the only way to reach God. They are right about that:

> I am the way, the truth, and the life. No one can come to the Father except through me (John 14:6).

But Christianity excludes no one. It is available to everyone who believes. It is totally inclusive. Even though God is intolerant of sin, He excludes no sinner from His free gift of salvation:

> For God so loved the world... (John 3:16).

> He [God] does not want anyone to perish (2 Peter 3:9).

*7. The skeptics object, "Christians are a bunch of hypocrites."* This is a legitimate criticism by skeptics. By and large, we Christians are a bunch of hypocrites. We talk about love and forgiveness, but we are often caught being spiteful and judgmental. But that is a criticism about us; it isn't a valid excuse for rejecting Christ. The fact that God loves us despite our imperfections (and our continual failings) illustrates God's grace.

By giving you a few answers to some tough questions skeptics ask, we aren't implying that you are going to have an easy time of it. Dealing with these issues takes study, prayer, and patience. Just remember that God has given you His Word and the Holy Spirit to help you give answers to anyone who asks you about the hope that's within you.

At the same time, you may have some tough questions of your own. That's perfectly natural. When your own doubts come up, you need to talk to God and to other believers. Christianity is not an individual sport; it is played as a team. The New Testament refers to Christians as being members of a family or as being different parts of the same body.

We think you will have a completely different perspective about Christianity when you learn to talk with God and other Christians about the things that are weighing you down. You'll realize a completely different, dynamic aspect of the Christian life. You'll know God is with you to comfort and guide you, and He'll be using other Christians to encourage you. When this happens in your life, you'll be truly excited about God. You won't have to fake it anymore. Your faith and trust in God will be genuine—and you'll be glad to tell others about it.

## A Few Things You Shouldn't Forget

Before we leave you, there are a few things we want you to remember:

- You aren't responsible for persuading or convincing people to accept Christ. You are just responsible for telling them about Him.

- This whole witnessing thing isn't even about you. And it isn't even about the person you are talking to. It is about Jesus. He is supposed to be the center of your attention.

- People can learn a lot about what you really believe by the way you live your life.

- You'll get better at sharing your faith the more often you do it.

# What's That Again?

1. Living your faith is much harder than explaining it.

2. You have the opportunity to live your faith in front of two kinds of people every day: the people you know and the people you don't.

3. Effective witnessing involves a combination of your character, your conduct, and your communication. Witnessing is all about telling and showing others what Jesus is like.

4. As Christians, our goal should be to be more like Christ in our thoughts, deeds, and words. This is a process that involves pursuing the character of Christ, practicing the deeds of Christ, and presenting the simplicity of Christ.

5. Sharing your faith effectively should be the natural outgrowth of loving God.

6. Skeptics can be intimidating, but once you understand that skeptics are simply seekers with tough questions, you will find plenty of reasons to share your faith with them.

7. The objections and questions about Christianity fall into a few basic categories. Once you do your homework and get a handle on how to respond, you will have much more confidence as you share your faith with seekers and skeptics alike.

## Dig Deeper

These two books discuss the practical aspects of sharing your faith:

*How to Give Away Your Faith* by Paul Little. This book is the classic. You'll find it very helpful.

*Out of the Salt Shaker & into the World* by Rebecca Manley Pippert. This book explains how we can build relationships that will allow us to share our faith with credibility.

And here are two excellent resources for dealing with the questions of skeptics:

*The Case for Christ* by Lee Strobel. With a background as a law scholar and journalist, Strobel was skeptical as he examined the evidence about Jesus. At the end of his investigation, he was convinced that Jesus was the Son of God. (Big surprise.)

*Finding Common Ground* by Tim Downs. This book includes practical discussions for finding ways to discuss spiritual matters in the context of everyday life.

# Questions for Reflection and Discussion

1. What if someone were to describe you as a "Sunday only" Christian? What would that mean? List three benefits to living your life as a "seven days a week" Christian.

2. Even though you have many opportunities to share your faith with the people you know, why is it hard sometimes for your friends and family to take your words to heart?

3. What does it mean to have the same attitude as Christ? How should that change the way you treat people?

4. What does it mean to practice the deeds of Christ? What could you do right now that would demonstrate this to another person?

5. List three benefits to loving God more. In what practical ways can you love God more than you do now?

6. Think of the people you know. List the names of three seekers and three skeptics (you don't have to share these names). How often do you see each of these people? In what ways could you be more intentional about sharing your faith with these six people?

7. What is the toughest question you have ever been asked about your faith? How did you answer it? What is the toughest question you've ever asked? Did you ever receive a satisfactory answer?

◻ ◻ ◻

## Moving On...

Sharing your faith is primarily a matter of *living* your faith. As you are in conversation with other people, witnessing is nothing more than simply talking naturally about the spiritual dimension of life. If you can share your excitement about watching a basketball game, or seeing a good movie, or eating at a great restaurant, we know that you can talk about God and what He has done for you.

As you begin to share your faith, you will get more excited about your relationship with God. And as your love for God grows more intense, you'll want to talk about Him even more. When you get that cycle going in your life, finding the words to say and the courage to speak will not be a problem for you anymore.

In the next chapter we're going to move to a new topic: the church. If you've ever felt like you're out there on your own, struggling to share your faith with others but not feeling the support of other believers, then perhaps you haven't found a church where you can both grow and help others grow in their Christian lives. As you're going to see in the next two chapters, going to church isn't just a good idea. It's God's idea, and it's where He wants you.

# Chapter 9

> The church is like a great ship pounded by
> the waves of life's various stresses.
> Our job is not to abandon ship,
> but to keep it on its course.
>
> *Boniface*

It is said that more people go to church each week than to any other single activity. We may live in an increasingly secular culture, but church remains a popular place for people to routinely gather in order to connect with each other and with God. Why is that? What is the great appeal of church, and why are there so many different kinds? Is one church better than another, or are they all pretty much the same? And is it necessary for a growing Christian to go to church, or is attendance optional?

In chapter 10 we will explore reasons why you should go to church and what you should expect—and what God expects of you—once you're there. But first we need to define what the church is, where it came from, and how it's supposed to function. That's what this chapter is all about.

# Church: It's God's Great Idea

## What's Ahead

- ☐ What Is the Church?
- ☐ Metaphors for the Church
- ☐ A Brief History of the Church
- ☐ Which Church Is the Best?

*D*rive down any street in any given town or city, and you're likely to see a huge variety of churches. You'll find denominational churches such as Baptist, Christian, Methodist, Presbyterian, Pentecostal, Lutheran, Covenant, Episcopal, Catholic, Reformed, and Evangelical Free. And you'll find nondenominational churches with words like *Community, Bible,* or *Fellowship* in their names.

Usually when we think of a particular church, we picture a building and a location. Some church buildings are beautiful and spread out on a campus, while others were once used as warehouses or stores. Some churches are made of brick and have a steeple, while others resemble a gymnasium. Some churches worship on Saturdays, while most meet on Sundays. A few megachurches meet several times throughout the week. Most churches, however, are relatively small.

*T*here are approximately 330,000 churches in America, with an average attendance of about 90 per church. But 32 percent of all men and 44 percent of all women say they attend church on a weekly basis.

And then there's the way churches worship. Walk into some churches, and you will experience a traditional service with an organ, hymns, and a preacher delivering his sermon from behind a pulpit. Other churches feature contemporary worship with guitars, praise choruses, and a pastor delivering a message as he walks back and forth on a stage.

## What Is the Church?

So just exactly what is the church? Is it everything we've described, or is there one simple definition? The answer is yes to both questions. The church is very diverse, but it is also very simple. Even more importantly, the church is not some human idea or invention. The church is God's great idea.

### The Meaning of Church

Even though you probably go to a specific place to worship God and study His Word, the definition of *church* is much broader than a particular location. In reality, the church includes all Christians—those who believe in the God of the Bible and have received Jesus Christ as their personal Savior—for all time. In other words, all Christians living today are part of the church, but so are all believers who have died.

### The Church Is Invisible and Visible

Because the church includes all genuine believers for all time, and because it is more than a collection of buildings and groups of people, there is a sense in which the church is *invisible*. From our human perspective, we don't know for sure who the true believers are, even in the church we attend. That's because we can't see people the way God sees them. Only God knows the true condition of the heart (2 Timothy 2:19). As theologian Wayne Grudem states,

*The invisible church is the church as God sees it.*

At the same time, the church is definitely *visible*. When we claim to be Christians and give evidence of our faith in our lives, then we can rightly say we are members of God's church. Professing Christians are the visible representative of the church. Here's the way Grudem puts it:

*The visible church is the church*
*as Christians on earth see it.*

Keep in mind that the visible church will always include some unbelievers. This doesn't give us the right to question the faith of others, and we certainly should not become suspicious (remember 2 Timothy 2:19).

---

# *T*he Church Belongs to God

The word *church* means "belongs to the Lord." The New Testament writers used the word *ekklesia* to describe a group of people who were "called out" by God. In the Old Testament, the nation of Israel was referred to as a group of people "called out" by God, so in a sense there was a church before Jesus came to earth. But the church we know today came into existence with the coming of Christ. Jesus lived and died for the church (Ephesians 5:25), and He has promised to build the church (Matthew 16-18) by calling people to Himself through salvation (Acts 2:47). Jesus began calling out people to Himself when He chose the original 12 disciples. Think of these 13 men as a little church that eventually experienced explosive growth on the Day of Pentecost, when the Holy Spirit first came in power to all believers (Acts 2:1-42).

---

## The Church Is Local and Universal

The word *church* can apply to local groups, whether they meet in special buildings, homes, or even outdoors. And it can also apply to the universal church, which is the church throughout the world. The bottom line is that those who have been called out by God at any level are part of the church.

## Metaphors for the Church

To help us understand the true nature of the church, the Bible gives us several helpful metaphors and images. Here are three that relate to the three persons of the Trinity:

- *The people of God.* We talked about this image when we said the church is made up of those who are "called out" by God. In the history of salvation, God has always called out people for Himself, for His purpose, and for His glory. In the Old Testament, God called out the Hebrew nation, and since Christ came to earth, God's church has been "grafted" like branches onto the plan God has for the people who belong to him (Romans 11:17-18). The church can also be called the *family* of God. As believers, God is our heavenly Father (Ephesians 3:14), and we are His sons and daughters (2 Corinthians 6:18).

- *The body of Christ.* This is the apostle Paul's favorite metaphor for the church, and he uses it in two ways. First, the body of Christ is the church as a body with various parts or members (foot, hand, ear, and eye) that function together for service. This part of the metaphor emphasizes the diversity and mutuality of the church. We all have different gifts and we all need each other (1 Corinthians 12:12-17). The other way Paul uses the metaphor emphasizes the unity of the church. We are all one body, and Christ is the head (Ephesians 1:22-23; 4:15-16).

- *The temple of the Holy Spirit.* A temple is a physical place where God dwells. The church is like that because it is the place where God dwells with His people through the Holy Spirit. This happens to each of us individually (1 Corinthians 6:19) and to the church corporately (1 Corinthians 3:16).

## A Brief History of the Church

You might be tempted to skip over this section (after all, it is about history), but we would urge you to take this whirlwind tour of the 2000-year history of the church. Knowing where the church came from will give you a greater appreciation for where the church is today. We're going to divide this section into three periods in church history: the ancient church (5 B.C. to A.D. 590), the church in the Middle Ages (590 to 1517), and the modern church (1517 to the present).

### The Ancient Church (5 B.C. to A.D. 590)

The church as we know it began with Jesus Christ. By God's grace and faith in Him, we are saved from sin, adopted into God's eternal family, and baptized by the Holy Spirit into the body of Christ. Christianity and the church cannot exist apart from the life, death, and resurrection of Christ.

### The Apostles and the Early Church

After His resurrection and before His ascension, Jesus gave His followers a set of instructions known as the Great Commission:

> *But when the Holy Spirit has come upon you, you will receive power and will tell people about me everywhere— in Jerusalem, throughout Judea, in Samaria, and to the ends of the earth* (Acts 1:8).

The early church followed these marching orders to the letter. The first 12 chapters of Acts tell us how the Good News message of Jesus was first proclaimed in Jerusalem, where Peter preached on the day of Pentecost. Initially the early church was primarily Jewish as the message went from Jerusalem to Judea and Samaria. Then, beginning in Acts 13, the apostle Paul followed the Lord's personal instructions: "Take my message to the Gentiles and to kings, as well as to the people of Israel" (Acts 9:15). Through the tireless efforts of Paul and the other apostles, the Gospel (that's the Good News) went to every corner of the known world.

---

*T*he word *apostle* means "sent ones." The original apostles knew Jesus firsthand and were sent by Him to preach the Good News. Later, other followers of Christ were also called apostles.

---

## The Apostolic Fathers

With the martyrdom of Peter and Paul in A.D. 64 and 68, the destruction of Jerusalem in A.D. 70, and the death of John at the end of the first century, the apostolic age came to an end. With all of the original apostles dead, the leadership of the church passed to the next generation, known as the Apostolic Fathers. Despite the persecution inflicted by Roman authorities during the second century, Christianity spread west from Antioch and across the Mediterranean to Northern Africa. Two of the most prominent Apostolic Fathers, Ignatius and Polycarp, were executed for their belief in Jesus Christ.

## Defending the Faith

As the truth about Jesus Christ spread, so did the error. Especially in the second half of the second century, false teaching—also known as *heresy*—crept into the church. The greatest threats were *Gnosticism* and *Monarchianism*.

- *Gnosticism.* This heresy had a dualistic view of reality. For the Gnostic, the intrinsically evil material world and the intrinsically good immaterial world were totally separate. It was impossible for a good God to create an evil, material world. Furthermore, it was inconceivable that Jesus could have had a physical body. Therefore, there could be no bodily resurrection.

- *Monarchianism.* This ancient form of Unitarianism emphasized the unity of God to such an extent that it opposed any attempt to conceive of God in three Persons. In effect, the Monarchians denied the real deity of Christ. He was not divine but merely a good man.

To combat these and other heresies, a new group of Christian leaders called *apologists* emerged in the second and third centuries. They were called apologists because they defended the truth about Christianity (the Latin word *apologia* means "defense"). The apologists used their writings to mount a defense on two fronts:

- *The apologists defended the faith against heresy.* Irenaeus (ca. 130–ca. 200) was the greatest defender against heresy. He argued that Scripture had true authority and that Jesus fulfilled Old Testament prophecies. Irenaeus taught that Jesus Christ and His bodily resurrection were the very core of Christianity.

- *The apologists defended the faith against the state.* From 100 to 250, the Roman government was increasingly hostile to Christianity, considering it a false religion. Justin Martyr (ca. 100–ca. 165) became the chief Christian apologist to the heads of state. He portrayed Christianity as a true and reasonable belief system worthy of acceptance by the Roman government.

## Peace at Last

At the beginning of the fourth century, the persecution of the church was still pretty bad, but there was some hope. The Roman Empire was ruled by two imperial leaders—Galerius in the east and Constantius Chlorus in the west. Galerius was determined to wipe out Christianity, but Constantius stopped the persecution of Christians in his realm. His son, Constantine, assembled an army to capture Rome from the eastern powers. When he encountered his opponent at the Milvian Bridge just outside the walls of Rome, Constantine turned to the Christian God for help. In a vision he saw a cross with the words, "In this sign conquer." He took this as a sign to advance, and he subsequently defeated the enemy and took control of the Roman Empire. In 313 Constantine issued the Edict of Milan, officially ending all persecution against Christians.

## Orthodox Theology

Finally, after more than 200 years filled with persecution, Christians were able to take a breath and tend to a very important issue: what they believed. When you live in a culture where it's illegal and downright dangerous to practice your faith, it's difficult to think about the details of your belief. You either believe in

Jesus or you don't. But when the pressure of persecution is lifted, you tend to look deeper into your beliefs. This is what Christians in the fourth and fifth centuries did. They defined what it meant to have orthodox theology.

---

*T*heology comes from two Greek words: *theos,* which means God, and *logos,* meaning word or rational thought. In essence, theology is rational thought about God. *Orthodox* theology is good or correct theology.

---

From 313 to 481, several theological controversies erupted and resulted in four major church councils (like our modern-day conventions). The purpose of these councils was to resolve the conflicts by forming creeds, or statements of belief. Although there were several issues, the core of the debates centered on the person, the nature, and the essence of Jesus Christ. Four major church councils met over a period of 150 years in order to correctly understand the true person of Christ.

- *The Council of Nicea (325).* As the Roman emperor, Constantine called the first council to deal with the controversy concerning the divine nature of Christ. Three positions were presented at Nicea:

  - Jesus was of a *different* essence from God the Father (this was the position of Arius),

  - Jesus was of the *same* essence as God (this was the position of Alexander and Athanasius), and

  - Jesus was of a *like* essence to the Father (this was a compromise position).

  The result of Nicea was that Arius was condemned as a heretic and Jesus was declared to be of the *same* essence as the Father. The Nicene creed said that Jesus is "true God from true God." Furthermore, in opposition to Arius, who taught that Jesus was created, the council of Nicea proclaimed Jesus as "begotten, not created."

- *The Council of Constantinople (381).* Another debate centered on the humanity of Christ. Just as Nicea declared Jesus to be fully God, Constantinople declared Jesus to be fully human. The council had to refute a heresy promoted by Apollinarius, who taught that Jesus wasn't completely human. The position of Constantinople was this: "The word of God has become flesh."

- *The Council of Ephesus (431).* Once the two natures of Christ were fully defined, another conflict arose: How do the two natures of Christ interact? A view called Nestorianism taught that the two natures had to be completely distinct and could never mix. Yet Scripture clearly teaches that Jesus' two natures were in a perfect relationship. Therefore, this council refuted Nestorianism and insisted on the unity of Christ's person. In other words, Christ was one person with two natures (a concept known as the "hypostatic union").

- *The Council of Chalcedon (451).* This council also confronted an issue concerning the natures of Christ, only this time they had to deal with a position called Monophysitism. Promoted by a monk named Eutyches, this view saw the two natures of Christ as one with no clear distinction. Chalcedon came up with this orthodox position: The two natures of Jesus are joined in one person without confusion, change, diversion, or separation. The reason this is so important is that our salvation depends on it. Jesus died and was resurrected as both God and man. As God He saved us, and as man He identified with us.

We need to be thankful for the hard work done at these councils by people who cared deeply about correctly stating the truth of their faith. Whether they were dealing with the nature of Christ or the reality of the Trinity, their focus always remained on the deity and the redemptive work of the Lord Jesus Christ. They showed us that the church has always been—and forever will be—about Jesus.

### The Church in the Middle Ages (590–1517)

Many people think of the Middle Ages—also known as the medieval era—as the Dark Age. Nothing could be further from the truth. Historians agree that the medieval period provided the very foundation of Western thought—both in philosophy and theology. Several other significant advances occurred at this time:

- Augustine and Aquinas produced their writings.

- The university was born.

- The great cathedrals of Europe, representing some of history's greatest architectural wonders, were designed and constructed.

- The printing press, which led to a flowering of literacy and knowledge, was developed.

Culturally, the church had a huge influence on how people lived. As we will see, there were abuses as the church gained more and more power, but the overall benefit to society was profound. There was no such thing as a secular culture. If you lived in the Middle Ages, you lived your life fully aware of the one true God.

### The First Medieval Pope

The reason the year 590 is usually considered the beginning of the Middle Ages is because this was the year Gregory I (also called the Great) became the bishop of Rome (he refused the title of Pope). The Roman Empire had collapsed, leaving a vacuum that was filled by the Roman Catholic Church and its new leader. Gregory the Great was a strong advocate of Scripture as the measure for life, and he encouraged missionary activity throughout the world.

### The Rise of Islam and the Crusades

During the seventh century and later, Christianity was confronted with a new monotheistic faith—Islam. Founded by Muhammad (570–632), Islam was based on a series of revelations

Muhammad claimed to receive from the angel Gabriel. The reve-lations were eventually collected in a new scripture called the Qur'an (Koran).

*T*he central teaching of the Qur'an and Islam is that there is one God, Allah, and Muhammad is his prophet.

Islam spread quickly as Muhammad preached faith in Allah. In 622 Muhammad and his followers were forced to flee to Yathrib (later renamed Medina, "the city of the prophet"). This flight to Medina, known as the Hegira, marks the beginning of the Islamic calendar and is considered the most important event in Islamic history. By 630 Muhammad had gained control over most of the Arabian peninsula. Within a hundred years, his suc-cessors had conquered Palestine, northern Africa, and Spain.

Arabs dominated Islam until the eleventh century, when the Seljuk Turks took over. Much more fanatical than the Arabs, the Turks harassed Christians making pilgrimages to Jerusalem, and they threatened the security of the Eastern church. In 1095, Pope Urban II issued a call to deliver the holy places of Palestine from Muslim control, officially kicking off the Crusades. As church historian Earle Cairns writes, "The whole movement may be characterized as a holy war against the enemies of the cross by the spiritual forces of Western Christendom." There were seven major crusades, but the First Crusade was the only successful one. The liberation of Jerusalem in 1099 and the creation of feudal states were the main results.

### Christianity as a Reasonable Faith

Throughout the history of the church, there has always been a tension between faith and reason: Is the Christian faith a blind leap in the dark, or is it rational? We can thank a group of medieval theologians known as the Scholastics for affirming the rational aspects of Christianity. Two of the most important Scholastics were Anselm of Canterbury (1033–1109) and Thomas Aquinas (1225–1274). Anselm ushered in a new era of Christian

## Meanwhile, in the Holy Roman Empire

The Roman Empire was revived in the West when Pope Leo III put a crown on the head of Charlemagne on Christmas Day in 800, creating a true Christian regime called the Holy Roman Empire. Eventually the church was divided into five regions: four in the East and Rome in the West. Because the Roman Church insisted on building its authority on the *papacy*, a major split occurred in 1054 between the Roman Church and the four Eastern regions, creating the Roman Catholic Church in the West and the Orthodox Church—which believed that the authority of the church needed to continue through apostolic succession—in the East.

thought when he showed that truth and reason are inseparable. He didn't say that we must come to faith through reason alone, but reason can be used as a way to better understand what we believe by faith. Anselm considered it a "sin of neglect" when someone who believes in Jesus Christ by faith does not strive after knowledge.

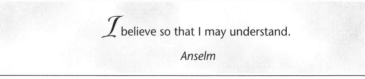

*I* believe so that I may understand.

*Anselm*

Aquinas was a brilliant theologian who developed a comprehensive doctrine of God (a doctrine is a set of ideas taught to people as truthful and correct), including the classic rational "proofs" for the existence of God.

## Crisis and Corruption

During the fourteenth and fifteenth centuries, the Roman Catholic Church experienced two things that paved the way for the Reformation: a crisis of leadership and increased corruption and fraud. Immorality and greed among many church leaders undermined their authority. It was common for clergy to buy and sell church offices (a practice known as *simony*). Even worse, the church raised money by selling holy relics (called *indulgences*) in exchange for forgiveness of sin and a reduced time in purgatory. Adding to the church's problems, mystic writers such as Thomas à Kempis were influencing people to hunger for a more personal, experiential type of Christianity. This flew in the face of the church's formalized and rigid ways.

Beginning in the fourteenth century, several prominent people were openly disagreeing with the Roman Church and calling for reform. John Wycliffe (1330–1384), an English reformer, boldly questioned papal authority, church hierarchies, and other Catholic practices. He believed that the only way to overcome abusive authority was to make the Bible available to everyday people in their own language (until then the Bible was available only in Latin, and only church leaders could read it). Wycliffe was convinced that if people could read Scripture for themselves, they would understand how they could have a personal relationship with Jesus Christ without going through the church. He was the first to translate the Latin Bible into English. By the sixteenth century, church reform seemed inevitable. All that was needed was a strong leader.

### The Modern Church (1517 to the Present)

The strong leader was Martin Luther (1483–1546), generally considered the father of the Protestant Reformation. Luther was educated in the finest Roman Catholic schools and became both a monk and a priest. As he studied the Scriptures, however, he became increasingly disillusioned with Roman Catholic practices, particularly the sale of indulgences for forgiveness of sin. Luther was convinced that pardon for sin came through faith alone *(sola fide)*. Works had nothing to do with it. And he believed that the Bible alone *(sola scriptura)* is the source of final authority and truth. By 1516 Luther was teaching that our inward righteousness is the gift of God and the source—rather than the result—of good works.

## The Reformation

On October 31, 1517, Luther went public with his arguments against the sale of indulgences by posting the 95 Theses on the door of the Castle Church in Wittenberg, Germany. Luther wasn't intending to create a whole new movement. He simply wanted to reform certain abuses that had negative consequences for morality and faith. Among other things, he argued that indulgences could not remove guilt, did not apply to purgatory, and provided a false sense of security. He also rejected the practice of transubstantiation, a belief that the bread and wine become the actual blood and body of Christ during Communion.

Essentially the theses were an invitation to debate the issues publicly (that was the protocol back then). But no one wanted to debate Luther, mainly because most of the professors and students at Wittenberg agreed with him. Instead, someone translated the theses into German and circulated them. As Luther's beliefs spread throughout Europe, the Reformation caught on like wildfire. Other leaders, such as the Swiss reformers Ulrich Zwingli and John Calvin, gained followers with their own theological interpretations. In fact, Calvin's influence was so strong that he inspired the Dutch Reformation and the English Reformation, as well as the Puritans who sailed to the New World in search of religious freedom a hundred years later.

## The Catholic Counter-Reformation

The energy and the commitment of the Protestant Reformers (they were called that because the reformers were seen as protesting the teaching and practices of the Catholic Church) put Catholicism on the defensive. Under the leadership of Pope Paul III, a Counter-Reformation began. For 18 years—from 1545 to 1563—a group of bishops met 25 different times at the Council of Trent to craft a response. The council acknowledged some of the abuses and established new guidelines for clergy.

# The Impact of the Reformation on Culture

Church historian Earle Cairns explains how the Reformation impacted culture in positive ways:

- It helped to create a demand for universal elementary education, because if people were to interpret the Bible for themselves, they must be able to read.

- Its insistence on spiritual equality motivated people to seek political equality.

- It promoted the rise of democracy in both the church and the state.

- It stimulated capitalism.

However, Trent rejected justification by faith alone and emphasized the need for works in order to be saved. Furthermore, the council reaffirmed transubstantiation and declared that church tradition had equal authority with Scripture. These declarations did nothing to bring about a reconciliation between Catholics and Protestants.

## Protestantism Gets Cold

Protestantism flourished in the sixteenth century, but by the seventeenth century it had become cold and impersonal. Christianity was little more than a set of beliefs, and churches weren't instructing people on how to live those beliefs in everyday life. As you would expect, the chilly condition of Protestantism produced two main reactions. One was *rationalism,* a philosophy that says the only way to know truth is through reason. In religious terms, this led to *deism,* which is basically a religion of reason.

# Deism and Its Consequences

The deist believes that God created the universe, but He isn't involved with it. In fact, God left His creation to operate by natural laws. The world as we know it doesn't include the supernatural (such as miracles), the Bible is not God's revealed Word, and Jesus is not the Incarnation of God Himself. He was simply a moral teacher who insisted that God alone was worthy of worship. Because deism ignored human sin, it was very optimistic about man's goodness and potential to achieve greatness—even perfectibility. Deism became the belief of choice of many of America's founding fathers, such as Franklin, Jefferson, and Thomas Paine (who wrote a book called *The Age of Reason* in 1795). According to Earle Cairns, modern liberalism, with its emphasis on rationalism, owes much to deism. Deists also led to the modern system of "higher criticism" of the Bible, which strips the Bible of the supernatural.

## Revivalism Takes Hold

The other reaction to cold Protestantism was *revivalism,* which emphasized the importance of the Bible and living out its teachings in everyday life. Quakerism, founded by George Fox (1624–1691) in England, stressed personal experience and taught that the true freedom of Christianity was found in the Spirit—or "inner light"—something each person must follow in order to find God.

Methodism, founded by John Wesley (1703–1791), also in England, taught that the Gospel should impact culture. To do this he trained lay preachers (including women) to spread the salvation message across the British Isles to the American frontier, where it flourished. Wesley personally traveled over 200,000 miles on horseback as he preached 42,000 sermons. His brother, Charles, wrote more than 70,000 hymns.

## The Great Awakenings in America

The Methodist church laid the groundwork for revivals and growth in America in the eighteenth century. There were two Great Awakenings that impacted the emerging American culture in significant ways. The first Great Awakening began in the 1720s and was led by George Whitfield and Jonathan Edwards, a brilliant and powerful preacher who had a unique ability to combine the logic of the Gospel message with the emotion of the human heart. Out of the first Great Awakening came new denominations, such as the Baptists.

The second Great Awakening came after the American Revolution and affected the new nation even more than the first. Most significantly, it brought about a shift from a God-centered theology (taught by the reformers and the Puritans) that stressed God's sovereignty and man's inability to save himself, to a man-centered theology that emphasized man's free will and ability in salvation.

## Evangelism and the Modern Mission Movement

It was only natural that the revivals and Great Awakenings of the seventeenth and eighteenth centuries would motivate Christians to take the Good News message of Jesus around the world. William Carey (1761–1834), considered the "father of modern missions," moved his family to Calcutta, India, in order to fulfill the Great Commission. His efforts there became a model for modern missions. J. Hudson Taylor (1832–1905) was a pioneer missionary in China, and others took the Gospel to previously unreached places, such as Africa. In America, evangelists such as D.L. Moody (1837–1899), Billy Sunday (1869–1935), and Billy Graham have preached the Gospel to untold millions of people in this country and throughout the world.

*Expect great things from God; attempt great things for God.*

*William Carey*

According to church historian James Eckman, "The achieve-ments of the modern missionary movement have been stag-gering." He lists six benefits:

1. Millions of people have found new life in Christ, and vir-tually every ethnic, racial, and language group is now rep-resented in the universal church of Jesus Christ.

2. Local churches now exist in just about every nation in the world.

3. Mission agencies have planted thousands of schools throughout the world.

4. Through its social and ethical integrity, Christianity has become a liberating force for women and other under-privileged groups in other cultures.

5. Christian mission agencies have built medical facilities and hospitals around the world to care for the medical needs of underprivileged people groups.

6. The Bible has been translated into hundreds of lan-guages through the efforts of missionary organizations.

## Which Church Is the Best?

With such a rich and varied history, you might be wondering if all churches today—including your own church—are true to God's original intention. Or you might be in the process of looking for a church to attend. How do you know which church is the best?

First of all, if you're looking for the best or the perfect church, you're going to be very disappointed. The only perfect church is the church God sees from His perspective—the invisible church. This is the church that's been called out by God Himself and made possible by the saving life of Christ. But the visible church—the one we can see—is far from perfect, mainly because it contains imperfect people. Rather than looking for the perfect church, you need to get involved with a growing church where the Word of God is preached and heard. And if you follow what

Martin Luther and John Calvin suggested, your church should practice the sacraments of baptism and the Lord's Supper.

Beyond that, we want to give you three "purposes of the church" suggested by theologian Wayne Grudem. We would agree that a church should be involved in these three things:

- *Worship*—this is a church's ministry to God.

- *Nurture*—this is a church's ministry to believers.

- *Evangelism*—this is a church's ministry to the world.

When a church keeps those purposes in balance, it will be in line with God's purposes for His people who are called by His name.

# What's That Again?

1. The church includes all Christians—those who believe in the God of the Bible and have received Jesus Christ as their personal Savior—for all time.

2. The word *church* means "belongs to the Lord." The church we know today came into existence with the coming of Christ to earth.

3. The invisible church is the church as God sees it. The visible church is the church as Christians on earth see it.

4. The church is local (the church you attend), and the church is universal (the church throughout the world).

5. The Bible gives us three images for the church that relate to the Trinity: The people of God, the body of Christ, and the temple of the Holy Spirit.

6. The ancient church (5 B.C. to A.D. 590) included the original apostles and the early church, the Apostolic Fathers, and the Apologists, who defended the faith against heresy. Once the persecution of the church stopped, the church was able to define orthodox theology through a series of councils.

7. The church of the Middle Ages (590 to 1517) had a pervasive impact on culture. Medieval theologians known as the Scholastics affirmed Christianity as a reasonable faith.

8. The modern church (1517 to the present) began with the Reformation, which strengthened the church and changed culture for the better. However, when Protestantism lost its fire, the church responded with revivals, spiritual awakenings, and a worldwide missions movement.

9. The true church is where the Word of God is preached and heard. A true church will worship God, nurture the believers, and evangelize the lost.

## Dig Deeper

The following books were helpful as we researched the purpose and the history of the church:

> *Christianity Through the Centuries* by Earle E. Cairns is arguably the best text on church history there is. It's full of information and insightful analysis.

> *Church History in Plain Language* by Bruce Shelley treats the history of the church more like a story. This book also looks at many of the current church trends, such as user-friendly worship services and the megachurch.

*Perspectives from Church History* by James Eckman is great because it's brief. It gives you thumbnail descriptions of every important event in church history.

Wayne Grudem's *Systematic Theology* includes several chapters on the purpose and the characteristics of the church.

# $\mathcal{Q}$uestions for $\mathcal{R}$eflection and $\mathcal{D}$iscussion

1. Describe the church you attend. Is it a denominational or a nondenominational church? Do you know anything about your church's history? Why did you choose to attend this particular church? If you don't have a church home, what would motivate you to start attending?

2. What's the difference between the visible and the invisible church? Why will we never be able to see the invisible church while we are on this earth? Why is this a good thing?

3. Will the Great Commission ever be fulfilled? Why or why not? Do you know of any places in our world today where the Gospel has not gone out?

4. Why is it important that the church guards against heresy? What does the Bible have to say about false teaching (see 1 Timothy 6:3-5; 2 Timothy 2:15-19; Titus 1:10-11)? What are two benefits of apologetics?

5. What is the correct view of the person and the two natures of Jesus Christ? Why must the church always be about Jesus?

6. Explain this statement: "Reason can be used as a way to better understand what we believe by faith." Give an example of how this has been true in your own life.

7. What's the difference between deism and Christianity? What are the consequences of believing in deism? What are the consequences of believing in Christianity?

## Moving On...

If you take nothing else from this chapter, we want you to understand two things. First, the church is God's idea, so it's a good idea for you to get involved. Second, the church will survive and thrive even when confronted with persecution, heresy, and complacency. God has always been about calling people to Himself through the church, and He will continue to do so until Jesus comes again.

Maybe you're still not comfortable in church. Perhaps you're a new Christian and the thought of going to church makes you nervous. Or maybe you've been to church and you had a bad experience. How should you get involved with a church, and what are you supposed to do when you get there? The next chapter is going to deal with these questions and more.

# Chapter 10

The Christian church is the only society in
the world in which membership is based
upon the qualification that the candidate
shall be unworthy of membership.

*Charles C. Morrison*

.

You can go to a lot of new places and feel comfortable on your first visit. Take a movie theater for example. You don't have any apprehensions about walking into a Cineplex for the first time. Oh, sure, you may not be familiar with the placement of the candy counter, and the knowledge of the restroom's location may evade you, but you have an overall confidence of what's going on and what you're expected to do: go in, sit down, shut up, and watch.

It isn't as simple with churches. It is understandable if you are nervous about going to a new church. Each one has its own peculiarities, and the differences go way beyond the location of the restrooms. Hey, most of them don't even have candy counters. (And here's another distinction: They usually don't use the word *lobby*. Every church will have one, but it will be described by a religious-sounding word like *vestibule, narthex,* or *foyer.*)

But you can't let your trepidation about going to a church keep you away. A lot goes on there that you need to be a part of.

# What to Do When You Go to Church

*C*hurches are like people. There are no two alike. Yes, there may be some striking similarities (particularly among churches within the same denomination), but a church's "personality" is primarily a reflection of the people who attend there. That's the most important part of any church—the people. Everything else (such as the type of music, the formality or informality of the unofficial dress code, and the activities during the worship service) is just a matter of style and preference. Don't get so focused on the logistics of any church that you overlook the character and quality of the people. If you find a place where the people reflect the character of Jesus and where the Word of God is preached, you're in a good place.

In the first few sections that follow, we want to give you an orientation of what you're likely to find when you go to a church. If you're a longtime churchgoer, none of this will surprise you. But if you're new to this church business, then you may find some helpful information about what going to church is all about. Most of all, we hope you come to understand that you need the church in order to grow as a Christian—and that the church needs you!

## Sitting, Standing, and Other Body Movements

Music, praise, and worship have always been vital parts of the Christian church experience. This pattern began back with the first small group of Christians in Jerusalem in about A.D. 33:

> *And all the believers met together constantly....They worshiped together at the Temple each day, met in homes for the Lord's Supper, and shared their meals with great joy and generosity—all the while praising God and enjoying the goodwill of all the people. And each day the Lord added to their group those who were being saved* (Acts 2:44-47).

Paul said that songs and praises are the natural response of a person who is filled with the Holy Spirit:

> *Let the Holy Spirit fill and control you. Then you will sing psalms and hymns and spiritual songs among yourselves, making music to the Lord in your hearts* (Ephesians 5:18-19).

In fact, Paul instructed the early Christians to enhance their worship of God by adding musical praises:

> *Use his words to teach and counsel each other. Sing psalms and hymns and spiritual songs to God with thankful hearts* (Colossians 3:16).

Don't be surprised when you walk into a church and find that music is a big part of the worship service. What may surprise you is the variety of worship styles. For example:

- *The traditional service.* Here you are likely to hear more hymns (Christian songs that may be centuries old and that usually have short melodies but several verses). These churches tend toward formality and may follow a program (called a *liturgy*) that involves congregational participation.

- *The Orthodox service.* Some Christian backgrounds prefer ancient traditions, usually from faraway countries. These services are rich with historic symbolism.

- *The contemporary service.* Here is where the style is informal and the music is usually very youth-oriented. The songs usually take the form of "praise choruses," many of which are verses of Scripture put to music.

- *The seeker service.* Some churches gear one or more services to the general public—those who might not be accustomed to going to church as a habit. These services tend to have less congregational participation because the intent is to provide an atmosphere where people can come as spectators to check out Christianity without feeling conspicuous.

Regardless of the style of worship service, congregations usually use some physical transitions. Don't worry about the rules—there aren't any.

- Don't worry about hand raising. It is simply a way some people express their praise and worship of God (usually during the musical portion of a service). Nobody is going to be bothered if you prefer to keep your hands in your pockets.

- You'll have a good idea of when to stand and when to sit by watching the other people around you. But don't think you can figure it out on your own. Sometimes a church might stand for the reading of some verses from the Bible, but other times the same church may read the Scriptures with everybody seated.

No one is going to make fun of you if you make some kind of movement faux pas. The people in the church are just glad you're there.

## Taking Communion

Go back and read Acts 2:44-47 as set forth on page 214. Notice that those early Christians celebrated the Lord's Supper. That still happens today in many churches, but it might be referred to in different terminology, such as "having Communion" or "partaking of the elements." Some do it every Sunday, and some do it once in a while. Some make a big deal out of it; others make it so intimate and personal that you might not know it is happening.

The act of Communion is basically a time to remember the fact that Christ died for our sins. It is called the Lord's Supper because it focuses on the event at the famous Last Supper that Christ spent with His disciples on the evening before He was crucified. The apostle Paul encouraged Christians to celebrate Communion with these words:

> For this is what the Lord himself said, and I pass it on to you just as I received it. On the night when he was betrayed, the Lord Jesus took a loaf of bread, and when he had given thanks, he broke it and said, "This is my body, which is given for you. Do this in remembrance of me." In the same way, he took the cup of wine after supper, saying, "This cup is the new covenant between God and you, sealed by the shedding of my blood. Do this in remembrance of me as often as you drink it." For every time you eat this bread and drink this cup, you are announcing the Lord's death until he comes again (1 Corinthians 11:23-26).

So there is symbolism in the bread and the wine. It is the fact of remembrance that is important, not any part of the procedure. Thus, some churches may use wine and unleavened bread; other churches may use grape juice and crackers.

## Being Baptized

Jesus wants His followers to be baptized. Baptism is not required for salvation, but it is an important part of the Christian faith because it marks a Christian's public profession of his or her association with Christ. Just in case you think this might not be a big deal, perhaps you should read some of Christ's last words to His disciples immediately before He ascended to heaven:

> *Jesus came and told his disciples, "I have been given complete authority in heaven and on earth. Therefore, go and make disciples of all the nations, baptizing them in the name of the Father and the Son and the Holy Spirit. Teach these new disciples to obey all the commands I have given you. And be sure of this: I am with you always, even to the end of the age* (Matthew 28:18-20).

Notice that Jesus views baptism as a natural part of the Christian experience. It is the way people make a public statement that they now belong to Christ.

Whenever baptism appears in the Bible, it takes the form of someone being immersed in the water. Yep, it is a dunking of the entire body. There is some good symbolism in this: When we accept Christ as Savior, our old nature dies (the "going under the water" part), and we become a new creature in Christ (the "coming out of the water" part).

Not all churches handle baptism the same way:

- Some do the dunking in an official baptistery in the church building.

- Some do the dunking at someone's backyard pool or in a lake, stream, or ocean.

- Some do the dunking by having the person fall back into the water, with the pastor helping to raise them back up on their feet.

- Some use a "squat down, pop up" technique.

- Others omit the dunking and use a sprinkling procedure.

Like praise and Communion, the logistics of baptism aren't as important as the statement that is made by doing it. If you're a Christian and have not yet been baptized, check into it (not because we said to, but because Christ said to).

## Giving Tithes and Offerings

Okay, now we're getting personal because we're talking about your money. Did you know that there is more written in the Bible about money than any subject other than God Himself? That isn't because Jesus wants your money. He doesn't need it. But you need to give your money as He directs to prove to yourself that you're looking to Christ—not your personal finances—to meet your needs.

There is a Christian term called *stewardship*. Many people mistakenly think that it applies only to money, but it is a much broader term than that. God wants you to be a trustworthy steward (manager) of all of the resources He has given to you, including your money, your time, your energy, and your creativity. All of those resources belong to Him, and you should be using them for His glory.

# What's a Tithe?

In Old Testament times, the Jews were required to regularly give a tithe (meaning "a tenth") of their income to God. (They were to make additional contributions on special occasions.) This tithe concept has carried over to modern Christianity, but there is no hard and fast rule about it. It's more like a rule of thumb. The better attitude is that that you should give whatever God asks of you. Be willing to give it all if that is what He wants you to do. That's why it is often called an offering: We are offering back to God what really belongs to Him in the first place.

Churches collect the tithes and offerings in different ways. Again, there is no right or wrong technique. It's just a matter of logistics. Some churches pass fancy bags down the rows, while others use plates. Some churches provide envelopes so you can mail your contributions, and others have a box at the back of the sanctuary.

Honoring God with your finances is an important part of your Christian walk. You could give financial assistance to any of the multitude of ministries that exist, but a principal place for your giving should be the church where you attend because that is the local congregation that is ministering to and through you.

## Putting Your Spiritual Gift to Work

Your involvement in a local fellowship of Christians—a church—is essential to your growing faith because that will be the place where you will find, exercise, and develop your spiritual gift. Remember back in chapter 2 when we discussed that a spiritual gift is given to you by the Holy Spirit for the purpose of helping others? You won't discover your spiritual gift, or be able to use it, if you keep to yourself and have no contact with other people. You need to get involved in some of the ministries of your church.

Volunteer to help out with some project. Be praying that God will help you identify your spiritual gift. It is not buried treasure. He wants you to find it and use it. Before long, you (and the people you are ministering with) may recognize that you have a special sensitivity or ability. That may be evidence of your spiritual gift.

Here's our final word on spiritual gifts: No one will benefit from your spiritual gift if you keep it under wraps. If you don't use it, the people around you will lose out on what the Holy Spirit can be doing for them through you, and you'll lose the benefit of seeing the Holy Spirit at work in your life in an obvious way.

# Is It a Talent or a Spiritual Gift?

There are several distinctions between your natural talents and your spiritual gift. Here are three important ones:

1. Your natural abilities come from your parents as a matter of genetics; your spiritual gift comes from God and is unrelated to the gene pool you're swimming in.

2. Your natural abilities are with you from birth (although a talent for belching your favorite song may not manifest itself until you are in junior high school). Your spiritual gift is apparently given at the time you put God in control of your life.

3. You can use your natural abilities and talents as you see fit, to benefit yourself or other people (or for evil purposes, if your knack is safecracking). Your spiritual gift is for the benefit of other Christians.

### Thanks, I Love It! What Is It?

Don't wait to get involved until you find your spiritual gift. It doesn't work that way. You'll have to be active in ministries of your church to see clues for what your gift might be. Of course, it doesn't hurt to know more about those gifts in advance.

In an attempt to help you define and compare the spiritual gifts listed in the four New Testament passages, we have placed them into five categories based on what the gift does. We don't know if anyone else categorizes spiritual gifts in this fashion, but it helps us make sense of them.

### Discerning Gifts—the Power to Know

- *Word of knowledge.* Did you ever wonder how Jesus knew certain facts about a person whom He never met before?

(See the story about His conversation with the woman at the well in John 4:1-42.) The spiritual gift of a word of knowledge is the supernatural ability to know some fact that would be impossible to know apart from divine revelation. This doesn't mean that you'll know all the information of the universe. God simply chooses to reveal a small bit of information that will be helpful in the situation, much like when the woman at the well believed what Jesus was saying because He knew certain things about her.

- *Word of wisdom.* This gift is a Holy Spirit-inspired revelation of a solution to an immediate problem. It is receiving God's wisdom for dealing with a particular situation. While all Christians are to study the Bible so we have a sense of God's wisdom (which is different from the world's value system), this spiritual gift is a special infusion of wisdom at a particular point in time for a particular purpose.

- *Discernment.* Similar to the gift of wisdom, the spiritual gift of discernment is an extraordinary ability to detect truth. It protects the Christian community from accepting false teachings. (We aren't supposed to leave the subject of God's truth to the people who have this spiritual gift. All Christians are instructed to study the Bible and test all teaching against what Scripture says.)

## Dynamic Gifts—the Power to Do

- *Faith.* Every Christian should have faith in God and His sovereign plan and power. The spiritual gift of faith, however, is the ability to believe God for the supply of a very specific need.

- *Miracles.* Jesus performed miracles to demonstrate that He was God's son. The apostles were given the authority to perform miracles to prove the authority of their message. God works miracles on His own, but He also gives some people the ability to perform miracles. Some scholars believe that this gift is primarily seen in parts of the world where the Gospel message is being presented for the first time.

- *Healing.* Certainly God can heal someone of a medical problem whenever He chooses to do so, and the New Testament instructs us on how to pray for healing. But there is a spiritual gift of healing as well. As with the gift of miracles, it may be that the primary purpose of this gift is to demonstrate the reality and authority of Jesus Christ.

## Declaring Gifts—the Power to Say

- *Prophecy.* In a general sense, *prophecy* refers to declaring God's message. In a technical sense, it refers to a specific message that God wants delivered to His people. There are many prophets mentioned in the Old Testament and a few in the New Testament.

- *Tongues.* This is the supernatural gift of being able to speak in a language that is not known to the person who is speaking it. The Day of Pentecost provides the best example of the demonstration of this gift. (See Acts 2:1-11.) This gift needs to be accompanied by the gift of interpretation (unless there happens to be some foreign-language-speaking person present who can translate). Often this gift is referred to as "praying in the Spirit."

- *Interpretation.* This gift is the ability to interpret the message being spoken in tongues so that the group can understand what is being said. Because the Christians in the church at Corinth were getting out of line with the gift of tongues, Paul instructed that no one was to speak in tongues unless the message could be interpreted. (See 1 Corinthians 14:27-28 for the circumstances that he imposed for the use of the tongues gift.)

## Discipling Gifts—the Power to Instruct

- *Apostleship.* An apostle is "one who is sent." In a technical sense, the term refers to the disciples who followed Christ while He was on earth, and then established the churches after Pentecost. Paul and Barnabas established churches also, and the term extends to them as well. Some scholars believe that this spiritual gift is not applicable now; others believe it may be found in those who are establishing churches around the world, just as early apostles did.

- *Pastoring.* This gift is a special ability to lead, care for, and protect the people in the local church. This is often referred to as "shepherding the flock" because the shepherd has the responsibility of leading, feeding, and protecting the sheep.

- *Teaching.* Many people are put in positions that require them to teach. If they have the spiritual gift of teaching, then they have a supernatural ability to explain the truth of God's Word in a way that is correct but also relevant, practical, and memorable.

- *Exhortation.* This is the ability to encourage people in their spiritual lives. Sometimes encouragement takes the form of supporting people; sometimes it means to admonish them. Either way, it involves spiritual sensitivity.

- *Evangelism.* Evangelism usually involves proclaiming the Gospel message to those who haven't heard it before. This spiritual gift is the ability to present God's salvation story with exceptional clarity in a way that helps people see their need for Christ. It is our guess that Billy Graham has the gift of evangelism.

## Disposition Gifts—the Power to Serve

- *Giving.* This gift has nothing to do with the amount of money you give. It involves unusual sensitivity to identifying special needs, along with overwhelming generosity with whatever means God has given to you.

- *Mercy.* All of us should be sensitive to the needs of other people. We should be available to comfort them in their times of trouble and discouragement. But most of us are oblivious to these circumstances, or we don't desire to help. A person with the gift of mercy has both the attitude and ability.

- *Serving.* Service may take many forms, but people with this spiritual gift have sensitivity for knowing how they can be of help to other people. More important than just knowing what to do, their gift empowers them to spring into action and get the job done. Usually, these acts of service are very practical.

- *Administration.* Being in a position of leadership doesn't necessarily mean that you have the gift of administration, but the gift sure would help you get the job done. This gift equips a person with good judgment and people skills for leadership in the church.

| Spiritual Gifts Given to Some | Commands Given to All |
|---|---|
| Service | Serve one another (Galatians 5:13) |
| Encouragement | Encourage one another (Hebrews 10:25) |
| Giving | Give generously (2 Corinthians 9:7) |
| Teaching | Tell others about Jesus (Matthew 28:19) |
| Mercy | Be kind (Ephesians 4:32) |
| Faith | Walk by faith (2 Corinthians 5:7) |
| Evangelism | Be a witness to others (Acts 1:8) |

Some gifts, such as faith and service, are qualities that every believer is required to have. In such cases the spiritual gifts of faith and service, for example, may be unusually strong capabilities in those areas.

Don't think that you can ignore every Christian activity that falls outside the parameters of your spiritual gift. You have certain responsibilities whether you have a spiritual gift in that area or not. Take witnessing, for example. You can't shirk Christ's command to tell others about Him with the lame excuse that "Hey, it's not my gift."

Keep in mind that a spiritual gift does not depend upon a position, role, or job. You don't have to be a pastor in your church to have the gift of teaching. And the pastor may actually have a spiritual gift other than those of pastoring or teaching. And

## What Spiritual Gifts Look Like in Action

We'll give you an oversimplified example of the spiritual gifts. Imagine that several people from your church are in a meeting. It has been going for a long while, and someone asks a young boy to bring a pitcher of water and some glasses into the room. The boy trips, and the pitcher of water spills all over the table. The spiritual gifts of each person in the room prompt them into immediate action:

- The person with the gift of service grabs a towel and starts mopping up the water.

- The person with the gift of mercy begins to comfort the distraught boy.

- The person with the gift of teaching shows the boy how to hold the pitcher so it won't spill next time.

- The person with the gift of encouragement tells the boy that he'll do better next time.

- And the person with the gift of leadership asks, "Who put this boy in charge of carrying the water?"

Okay, we're being a bit sarcastic, but you get the idea.

a spiritual gift is not a specialized technique. Someone in your church may be an expert at playing the piano or designing the church's website. These aren't spiritual gifts; they are just abilities that came through a lot of practice.

# What's That Again?

1. The essence of a church is not its style of worship but its people.

2. There are a variety of musical styles in churches. Find the one that best helps you praise God, because that is what worship is all about.

3. Churches vary in the way they handle the ordinances of Communion and baptism. The important point is not the way in which it is handled but the fact that Communion celebrates the sacrifice of Christ on the cross, and baptism allows a believer to make a public profession of his or her faith in Christ.

4. Churches get a bad rap for talking about money too much. That's only because too many Christians are too tight-fisted. God wants you to be a good steward of the money He has given to you, and financially supporting your church is an excellent way to get started with that.

5. You must be involved in a church because that's where you will discover and use the spiritual gift that the Holy Spirit has given to you.

6. Don't wait until you find your spiritual gift to get involved in a ministry. Get involved first, and your spiritual gift may become evident as you start serving others.

## Dig Deeper

Here are some resources for helping you make the transition from being a churchgoer to being an integral part of the church body.

> *Practical Christianity,* compiled by Tyndale House Publishers, is a collection of essays by various Christian authors. The chapter on "Life in the Church" has some great practical advice.
>
> A new classic is *The Purpose-Driven Life* by Rick Warren. Many church congregations have studied this book together. You'll get the idea that you weren't meant to live the Christian life disassociated from other believers.
>
> On the ordinances of the church (such as Communion, baptism, etc.) you might want to read a book on theology. We like *Basic Theology* by Charles C. Ryrie because it is written in short, understandable chapters. Look at the section entitled "I Will Build My Church."
>
> *Ministering Through Spiritual Gifts* by Charles Stanley. This study guide may help you discover and use your spiritual gift.
>
> There seems to be more confusion about the gift of praying in the Spirit than any other spiritual gift. *The Charismatic Gift of Tongues*, by Ronald E. Baxter, gives an objective approach to this subject.

---

# *Q*uestions for *R*eflection and *D*iscussion

1. What has been your church experience thus far in your Christian life? Has it been good or bad? What were some of the contributing factors?

2. Do you have a favorite style of worship? What do you enjoy about your favorite style? What elements can you appreciate about some of the other styles of worship?

3. Explain the importance and meaning of communion.

4. Have you been baptized? If so, describe what it meant to you. If not, state what you think might be holding you back.

5. Do you feel that God has control of your finances? Why is this subject so sensitive for many people?

6. Identify what you think might be your spiritual gift. Explain how it can be used to help others. If you don't yet know what your spiritual gift is, then describe some of the ministries in which you are involved in your church and what you like about them.

## Moving On...

As you grow in your faith, you'll find that you have an increasing desire to do God's will. You'll be in love with Him so much that you'll want to make sure that you are doing exactly what He wants you to do (and nothing else). And this is exactly where many Christians begin to get bogged down. They come to a screeching halt in their Christian growth because they can't seem to "find" God's will. What they don't realize is that they are looking too hard—because God's will is not that difficult to find.

# Chapter 11

To walk out of His will is to walk into
nowhere.

*C.S. Lewis*

Pity the poor people who have no faith in God. When they want to know the answers for their future, they are stuck with sources like the horoscope on the comics page of the newspaper. Or, if they have a credit card, they can talk to a phony phone psychic for $19.95 for three minutes. Or, if they are really desperate, they can consult the Magic Eight Ball. Whatever their decision, they are taking a stab in the dark. Without clear direction, we naturally worry about the decisions we made in the past and fret about the decisions we have yet to make about our future.

But Christians know the One who knows the future. We can go directly to Him for advice when we have big (or small) decisions to make. There is no better source for direction in our lives than God Himself. After all, since He knows everything and wants what is best for us, all we have to do is find His will for any decision that confronts us.

Sounds simple, but many Christians make it more difficult than it needs to be. In these final two chapters, we give you some guidelines about finding God's will for your life. As you learn to lock in on God's will, you'll discover both a purpose for your life and a great sense of freedom. And you can throw that Magic Eight Ball away.

# God's Will: Why Should You Care About It?

Our favorite part of eating Chinese food happens after the meal is over. Sure, some of the gastronomic delicacies are delicious, but the real thrill of Chinese dining comes when the dishes are cleared and everyone grabs for one of the shrink-wrapped fortune cookies. You know what we are talking about. There is a ceremony at the end of dinner when everyone cracks open his or her cookie. Few people actually eat the cookie (which has the flavor of a stale vanilla wafer and the consistency of an egg carton), but everyone takes a turn reading aloud his or her "fortune." Every strip of paper has a different message, but they usually center on a theme such as "Prosperity is headed your way if you show generosity to those who serve you." (It makes you wonder if the waiters themselves compose these sayings in an attempt to obtain bigger tips.)

There is something very interesting about Chinese fortune cookies. Everybody likes to read the "fortune," but nobody takes it seriously. It is not surprising that these wise-sounding prognostications are ignored. After all, consider the guy who wrote them:

- He has no idea who you are.

- He lacks any reliable insight into the future.

- He can't be trusted to help you have a successful life (because his own bleak existence consists of sitting in some windowless room for 18 hours a day cranking out 1500 fortunes on his 1980s IBM Selectric typewriter).

People don't laminate these fortunes to carry in their wallets. Those strips of paper are either wadded into a ball or used to dislodge chow mein that is stuck between their teeth. You aren't going to change your life based on that Chinese fortune cookie because you have no reason to believe its message.

By now you are probably wondering what Chinese fortune cookies have to do with finding the will of God. We don't blame you for wondering, but we are about to make a comparison between them. Actually, we think you'll be surprised that our analogy is so profound. (We surprised ourselves because it doesn't happen very often for us.) Here it is: *Unless you believe that God's plan for your life is reliable and relevant, it will be as meaningless to you as that fortune cookie.*

### Motivations for Finding God's Will

Before we explore the reliability and relevance of God's will, let's examine the variety of motivations that Christians have for trying to discover God's will:

- *Reverence.* By definition, a Christian has put God in control of his or her life. Doing whatever God says and going wherever He directs seems like the religious thing to do.

- *Curiosity.* Some Christians still want to call the shots, but they know it would be helpful to have a few clues about their future.

- *Confusion.* Maybe there is a current crisis going on. They need God's help to make a decision. Once He gets them past this rough spot, they'll take it from there.

- *Desperation.* Having made a mess of things so far, they go to God as a last resort.

Why do we bother asking about the motivations for seeking God's will? Well, your motivation may profoundly influence the way you respond to God's will when you find it. Here we go getting profound again: *Your desire to know and follow God's will is directly proportional to your belief that He knows what is best for you and is able to do something about it.*

If you are just mildly curious about God's will, or if you are only interested in it as a quick fix to get you out of a problem, then God won't have much more credibility for you than the fortune cookie writer. That perception of God (and your response to His will) is bound to change if you become convinced that God's will is relevant to your life and that it is entirely reliable.

In the sections that follow we will be reviewing the biblical foundation for why God is more trustworthy than a Chinese fortune cookie. As you will see, He knows all about you and your future, and He is intimately and actively involved in the details of your life. Finding and following God's will for your life makes sense because of who He is, what He knows, and what He wants to do for you.

## God Has What It Takes

When it comes to choosing your advisors, your options are rather bleak:

- Most of the people you know aren't much smarter than you are. They might be willing to offer you some advice, but you might do better on your own.

- Except for a few family members or friends, other people are more interested in their own welfare than in yours. Can you really trust their advice to be objective? (We've got three words for you: *used car salesman.*)

- You have to worry about the hype. Whether you are considering an investment, a career, or a move to another city, separating the truth from the propaganda complicates your decision. Is it too good to be true? How can you know for sure?

As you consider the plans for your life, wouldn't you prefer to go to an all-knowing source...someone like the Wizard of Oz? Well, God is everything that you need (and you won't be disappointed by finding some little guy hiding behind a curtain).

When you accepted Christ as your Savior, you did a good thing. That decision entitles you to eternal life. But there are benefits for the present too. You are now connected with God, who has all of the characteristics (called attributes) that are exactly what you would want from someone who is going to advise you with your day-to-day decisions.

### God Is Omniscient

God knows everything. All things past and all things future. He knows all things technical (like the chemical composition of DNA) and all things trivial (like the numbers of hairs on your head, which may not be trivial to a guy with a receding hairline). He knows you better than you know yourself.

> O Lord, you have examined my heart and know everything about me. You know when I sit down or stand up. You know my every thought when far away. You chart the path ahead of me and tell me where to stop and rest. Every moment you know where I am. You know what I am going to say even before I say it, Lord (Psalm 139:1-4).

If you are going to be looking to someone to guide you through life, this omniscience trait could prove to be very useful. Because God has all knowledge, His judgments are always made wisely. He sees all things in their proper perspective, and He is never surprised by new information that would require a change in His plans.

## *God Is Omnipresent*

He is everywhere, all at the same time. This means that you can't escape or hide from Him regardless of how hard you try. But it also means that He is always with you wherever you are.

> *I can never escape from your spirit! I can never get away from your presence! If I go up to heaven, you are there; if I go down to the place of the dead, you are there. If I ride the wings of the morning, if I dwell by the farthest oceans, even there your hand will guide me, and your strength will support me. I could ask the darkness to hide me and the light around me to become night—but even in darkness I cannot hide from you. To you the night shines as bright as day. Darkness and light are both alike to you* (Psalm 139:7-12).

Even if you have made poor decisions that have taken you down the wrong road in life, you can never get beyond God's presence.

## *God Is Omnipotent*

He is all-powerful. No person, nation, or confederation, whether of this earth or beyond, can conquer Him. He is able to do anything consistent with His own nature.

> *O Sovereign LORD! You have made the heavens and earth by your great power. Nothing is too hard for you!* (Jeremiah 32:17).

This aspect of God's nature is not limited to phenomena such as creating the world, navigating plagues of locusts, or walking on water. Amazingly, this power also affects human events. So don't abandon hope in God's plan just because someone is standing in the way; God can work effectively to change circumstances, whether your own or others'.

The extent of God's attributes is not exhausted with these three *omni* words. He has several other personality traits that make Him the perfect One to be in charge of your life planning. Keep reading.

## God Is Just

He is fair and impartial. He does not play favorites.

> *He is the Rock; his work is perfect. Everything he does is just and fair* (Deuteronomy 32:4).

There will be times when life seems unfair. If you are operating under God's plan, however, you can be assured that He is dealing equitably with you because that is the essence of His nature.

## God Is Holy

He is righteous. No fault is found in Him. His moral character is without flaw. There is not a bit of evil in Him; He is completely pure. In other words, He is wholly holy.

> *In a great chorus they sang, "Holy, holy, holy is the LORD Almighty! The whole earth is filled with his glory"* (Isaiah 6:3).

God's direction will never lead you down the wrong path. He can't go there Himself, and it is against His nature to direct you in error.

## God Is Love

God's love is not a romantic feeling (as Hollywood usually defines *love*). In contrast, God's love refers to unselfishness and commitment. He is ready to forgive, and He desires to be merciful toward you.

> *Dear friends, let us continue to love one another, for love comes from God. Anyone who loves is born of God and knows God. But anyone who does not love does not know God—for God is love* (1 John 4:7-8).

Because God loves you, He won't sabotage your life with some fiendish scheme because He is holding a grudge against you. God loves you and wants what is best for you.

### God Is Immutable

God doesn't change. His character is always the same—yesterday, today, and tomorrow.

*I am the LORD, and I do not change* (Malachi 3:6).

There are a lot of things that change unexpectedly and throw your life into turmoil, such as income tax changes, airline schedules, and your spouse's moods. But you'll never be surprised or disappointed with God's attitudes. You can plan your life around them.

## He's Got It All

Life is tough if you have to make all of your decisions by yourself. First, you've got to know the right thing to do. Then, you must have the determination to do it. (Even if we know what needs to be done, we may lack the desire or the discipline.) Finally, we need the ability to accomplish it.

With God's attributes, however, He is never frustrated over what to do, and He never lacks the desire or ability to get it done:

- He is wise, so He always knows what to do.

- He is good, so He always chooses to do the right thing.

- He is powerful, and therefore always capable of doing what He wills to do.

If you are seeking advice and direction as you pursue life as a Christian, aren't those the kind of character qualities you are looking for?

### God Is Running the Show

Imagine the apostle Paul and Charles Darwin arguing with each other on one of those cable television shows. Their conversation might go something like this:

Darwin:   There is no order in the universe. It is spinning randomly in space. Things just happen. There is no reason to it all.

Paul:     Hold on a minute, Chuck. God created the universe, and He is still in control of all that is happening in the world.

Darwin:   God? There is no God. And even if there were, he, she, or it had nothing to do with the earth. What happens here, happens by undirected, random chance. I'm so sure of that fact, I'd stake my life on it.

Paul:     I'm sorry to hear that.

In contradiction to Darwin's position, the Bible describes God as being *sovereign*. That means everything happens according to His will and plan. The Bible boldly and repeatedly declares that God is totally and completely in charge of everything.

> *The LORD does whatever pleases him throughout all heaven and earth* (Psalm 135:6).

God's sovereignty covers everything:

- from the big, cataclysmic occurrences in the universe (Revelation 4:11) to the miniscule details of your life (James 4:13-15), and

- from international politics (Proverbs 21:1) to your own physical, emotional, and psychological problems (1 Peter 3:17).

There is nothing in all of creation that is outside of God's sovereign control. (Since God created everything, it makes sense that He continues to control all of it.) Proverbs 16:33 even says that God determines the roll of the dice. (Caution: don't interpret this verse as a biblical mandate for gambling in Las Vegas. It says the Lord determines how the dice will fall, but it doesn't say He will make them fall in your favor.)

The sovereignty of God means that nothing happens in the universe—or in our lives—without God allowing it. Because He is sovereign, God is better at designing a plan for your life than you are. Think about it:

- Nothing ever catches God by surprise; it happens only if He allows it.

- There is nothing that He can't handle; everything is under His control.

- He doesn't worry about what will happen next; He knows everything in advance.

- He always has the correct response to the events that occur.

You probably can't say those things about yourself, so aren't you glad that you've got Someone on your side who is sovereign?

## Providence Is Not Just a City in Rhode Island

It is time for a little review:

- God is large (think of all of those *omni* words and the other attributes of God), and

- God is in charge (remember His sovereignty).

But an accurate understanding of how God operates in the world and in your Christian life gets a little more complicated because of one thing: you. You are a key player in what God is trying to accomplish *in* and *through* you, so any discussion about God's will has to deal with how you respond to it all.

Have you ever stopped to wonder how God interacts with humanity? Sure, He is large and in charge, but how involved is He in the day-to-day circumstances of your life? Does He pay attention to every little detail? Shouldn't the hole in the ozone layer and global warming involve more of His concentration than helping you decide which parking space to choose? Do you even want God to know about your facial blemishes when there are earthquakes and mudslides in Central America that need His attention?

Let's get even more personal. Beyond what God *knows* about you, how much does He get *involved* with the circumstances of your life? And do you consider His involvement to be a legitimate interest or an overbearing intrusion? Where does God's control stop and your personal freedom begin? Does one infringe on the other?

All of these questions relate to God's *providence*. Theologians use that term to describe God's continuing involvement in the daily events of the world (in general) and in your life (in particular) to bring about His intended results. God is not like some absentee landlord who never bothers to know what is going on with his property. God is not just a spectator-creator who brought you into this life and then left you to fend for yourself in the cold, cruel world with nothing but your own resources. (On the other hand, God is not some micromanager who manipulates every single event of your life so that you have no choice and are like a pawn in a celestial chess game.)

### God's Providence Means Our Preservation

There is a preservation aspect to God's providence. This involves protection and providing for needs.

- God's preservation applies to creation as a whole.

    *You alone are the LORD. You made the skies and the heavens and all the stars. You made the earth and the seas and everything in them. You preserve and give life to everything, and all the angels of heaven worship you* (Nehemiah 9:6).

- God's providence preserved the Israelites in the wilderness by providing them with manna, quail, and water.

- Jesus assured the disciples that they didn't need to worry about food or clothing because God handles that:

    *So I tell you, don't worry about everyday life—whether you have enough food, drink, and clothes. Doesn't life consist of more than food and clothing? Look at the birds. They don't need to plant or harvest or put food in barns because your heavenly Father feeds them. And you are far more valuable to him than they are* (Matthew 6:25-26).

• Jesus taught that God's providence protects us from being separated from God:

*My sheep recognize my voice; I know them, and they follow me. I give them eternal life, and they will never perish. No one will snatch them away from me, for my Father has given them to me, and he is more powerful than anyone else. So no one can take them from me* (John 10:27-29).

• The apostle Paul also explained that the providence of God preserves us from being separated from God:

*I am convinced that nothing can ever separate us from his love. Death can't, and life can't. The angels can't, and the demons can't. Our fears for today, our worries about tomorrow, and even the powers of hell can't keep God's love away. Whether we are high above the sky or in the deepest ocean, nothing in all creation will ever be able to separate us from the love of God that is revealed in Christ Jesus our Lord* (Romans 8:38-39).

God's providence doesn't preserve us from dangers or problems. God never promises that we will avoid tragedy, suffering, or persecution. In fact, following God usually involves a degree of hardship, but these allow us to identify with Christ's sufferings.

*Dear friends, don't be surprised at the fiery trials you are going through, as if something strange were happening to you. Instead, be very glad—because these trials will make you partners with Christ in his suffering, and afterward you will have the wonderful joy of sharing his glory when it is displayed to all the world* (1 Peter 4:12-13).

## God's Providence Governs Our Activities

Another aspect of God's providence is His affirmative and proactive involvement in guiding and directing the course of events to fulfill His purposes. This aspect is sometimes referred to as God's *governing* activity. His governing activity extends over

- the elements of nature (Psalm 135:5-7),

- the animal kingdom (Psalm 104:21-29),

- nations and governments (Daniel 2:21), and

- the circumstances of individuals (1 Samuel 2:6-7).

If you have always prided yourself on being an independent and self-sufficient person, what you've read so far in this chapter might have been hard for you to swallow. You might be getting a bit fatalistic at this point. You might be thinking that it doesn't matter what you do in life or what choice you make because God is calling all of the shots. After all, His sovereignty puts Him in control, and His governing activity has Him involved and active in all aspects of life. Is it beginning to look like your own thoughts and choices are pretty irrelevant to what's happening in your life?

Wait! Don't be misled. God's sovereignty and providence do not operate in a fashion that makes your input dispensable. The exercise of your free will is not precluded by God's will. Divine sovereignty and human freedom may seem completely contradictory on the surface, but that isn't how it works out.

Although God has the ability to intervene in all of the events of life, He does not dictate every occurrence that happens in your life. Much of what happens is just the natural sequence of events or due to the laws of nature. God does not always intervene. Oftentimes He just allows things to happen and refrains from tinkering with them. (To prove our point, pray that God will protect you from injury, and then drop a brick above your foot.)

This means that you can't assume that every single event in your life has been specifically directed by God's providence. So, don't read too much into the fact that you got a parking spot in front of Starbucks or that you've got a runny nose. Yes, within His sovereignty, God has allowed those things to happen, but maybe you just got the parking spot because you are lucky and maybe you've got a runny nose because of allergies. You can't attribute every circumstance in your life to God's intervention. You still have to be responsible for the consequences of your own decisions (and your own stupidity). Within the realm of God's sovereignty, He still allows you the freedom to make your own choices (and to experience the corresponding consequences).

## Your Will vs. God's Will

When you became a Christian, you didn't forfeit your free will. You still have it, and God doesn't want to take it away from you. Without it, you would be little more than a machine that works according to someone else's design and input. With your free will intact, you have the ability and the power to make decisions. Your determination and desire to do certain things—or not to do them—come from your will, and that's the way God wants it.

Before you accepted God's free gift of salvation, you had no desire for God, and you had no desire to know and to do God's will. But you voluntarily surrendered your will to God's will when you became a Christian. And that's the way God wants it. When you made the choice to follow God by believing in Jesus, God changed you into a new person. Because you responded to God in this positive way, He is at work changing your desires and shaping your decision-making processes.

> *God saved you by his special favor when you believed. And you can't take credit for this; it is a gift from God. Salvation is not a reward for the good things we have done, so none of us can boast about it. For we are God's masterpiece. He has created us anew in Christ Jesus, so that we can do the good things he planned for us long ago* (Ephesians 2:8-10).

But you aren't an automaton. You can still choose to reject God's leading in your life if you wish to do so. (You won't lose your salvation by such rebellion, but it certainly runs contrary to your desire to grow in your Christian faith.)

As a Christian, you've got the best of all possible situations:

- By your salvation, you have a new nature. You have been freed from the constraints and slavery of sin, you are truly liberated to exercise your free will in accordance with God's plan for your life.

- God wants you to know and experience His will for your life. And He'll give you the guidance and power to make it happen.

## God's Will—a Top-Ten List

Okay, here it is. The part you've been waiting for. We're going to tell you exactly what God wants you to do. We know with absolute certainty God's will for your life. The reason we can be so bold is that God has laid out His will in the Bible. Listed below are ten things that God has in mind for you.

Think of these as God's general will for you and all people everywhere. We know you've got some specific questions about issues that are personal to you, such as your education, your finances, your career, and your relationships. We'll cover finding God's will for the specifics of your life in the next chapter. But before you get to some specific circumstances, let's cover the overriding general principles of God's will. (Don't be intimidated by the list of ten. You've already got the first two items covered.)

*1. God wants you to believe in Jesus and accept Him as your Savior.*

This is number one on God's list of things He wants you to do. You checked this one off the list when you became a Christian. Contrary to what many people believe, God doesn't want anyone to die in their sins without knowing Him personally. (John 3:16 is proof of that.)

*2. God wants you to have eternal life.*

God created humanity to be in a relationship with Him—forever. Here again, this happened for you when you accepted Christ as your Savior. As Jesus said in John 6:40, "It is my Father's will that all who see his Son and believe in him should have eternal life."

# $\mathcal{T}$wo Down, Eight to Go

The first two on the list happened when you became a Christian. They are taken care of, permanently. But you are in process on the remaining eight, and you always will be. These eight are all parts of growing as a Christian.

*3. God wants you to be like Jesus.*

God doesn't want you to accept Jesus and then live your life as you previously did. His will for you is to be like Jesus, to live your life the way Jesus did, and to do the things that Jesus did.

> *Those who say they live in God should live their lives as Christ did* (1 John 2:6).

*4. God wants you to love Him.*

A lawyer once asked Jesus to identify the most important commandment. Here's what Jesus said:

> *"You must love the Lord your God with all your heart, all your soul, and all your mind." This is the first and greatest commandment* (Matthew 22:37-38).

*5. God wants you to love others.*

The interchange between the lawyer and Jesus continued and showed that the most important commandment actually has two parts. You can't have one without the other.

> *A second is equally important: "Love your neighbor as yourself"* (Matthew 22:39).

*6. God wants you to obey Him.*

Loving someone and doing what pleases them go hand in hand. Your love for God should compel you to want to do what He wants you to do.

> *Obey God because you are his children. Don't slip back into your old ways of doing evil; you didn't know any better then* (1 Peter 1:14).

*7. God wants you to change the way you think.*

It's so easy—even as a Christian—to get caught up in the way everybody else does things. God wants something much different from you, and it starts with changing your mental orientation. God wants you to start thinking in His paradigm.

> *Don't copy the behavior and customs of this world, but let God transform you into a new person by changing the way you think. Then you will know what God wants you to do, and you will know how good and pleasing and perfect his will really is* (Romans 12:2).

*8. God wants you to know Him better.*

Knowing God is a lifelong challenge that will enrich your life every single day. But God won't force Himself on you. It's up to you to learn more about God and what He wants you to do. Here's what the apostle Paul wrote to some first-century Christians:

> *We ask God to give you a complete understanding of what he wants to do in your lives, and we ask him to make you wise with spiritual wisdom. Then the way you live will always honor and please the Lord, and you will continually do good, kind things for others. All the while, you will learn to know God better and better* (Colossians 1:9-10).

*9. God wants you to submit to Him.*

As you become more like Christ each day, you will lead a moral, loving life that is in submission to God. This is a big part of God's will for your life.

> *The LORD has already told you what is good, and this is what he requires: to do what is right, to love mercy, and to walk humbly with your God* (Micah 6:8).

*10. God wants you to do His will.*

This may sound redundant, but think of this last principle as a summary of all the others. God wants you to think about doing His will all the time. The message that Moses gave to the people of Israel applies equally to us today:

*And now, Israel, what does the* LORD *your God require of you? He requires you to fear him, to live according to his will, to love and worship him with all your heart and soul, and to obey the* LORD*'s commands and laws that I am giving you today for your own good* (Deuteronomy 10:12-13).

# What's That Again?

1. Your desire to know and follow God's will is directly proportional to your belief that He knows what is best for you and is able to do something about it.

2. God is *omniscient* (all-knowing), *omnipotent* (all-powerful), and *omnipresent* (everywhere at the same time). These attributes make Him the perfect source for guidance.

3. By His sovereignty, God is in charge of what is happening in the universe and in your life. By His providence, God is intimately involved in the circumstances and details of your life.

4. God's sovereignty and providence don't incapacitate your own free will. You are free to choose to follow God's will or to ignore it.

5. The Bible gives us several general overriding principles for God's will. After we have followed His will that we accept Christ as Savior, then the others center on growing in our love and understanding of Him. It is God's will that we know and do His will.

## Dig Deeper

The more you know about the character of God, the better you'll feel about Him being in charge. Here are three books that are helpful in studying God's attributes: `

*Knowing God* by J.I. Packer. This book is considered a classic on the subject.

*Chosen by God* by R.C. Sproul. Dr. Sproul gives an excellent analytical explanation of God's sovereignty.

*Does It Matter If God Exists?* by Millard J. Erickson. This book explains who God is and what He has done for us. That understanding is a good foundation for pursuing God's will for your life.

On the more focused subject of God's will, we have these recommendations:

*Invisible Hand* by R.C. Sproul. Do things "just happen" in your life, or do they happen for a reason? This book gives the answer.

*The Will of God as a Way of Life* by Gerald L. Sittser. This is an extremely practical book that shows how God actively guides you in the present circumstances of your life.

*Affirming the Will of God* by Paul E. Little. A classic little booklet that makes a lot of sense.

---

# $\mathcal{Q}$uestions for $\mathcal{R}$eflection and $\mathcal{D}$iscussion

1. What is the correlation between your understanding of God's nature and your willingness to follow His will? (We give you

permission to use our "Chinese fortune cookie" analogy in your answer.)

2. Review each of the seven attributes of God. Explain why each one makes Him the perfect advisor for your life's decisions.

3. What is the difference between God's sovereignty and His providence? Why are these concepts relevant to the subject of following God's will?

4. What is the concept of God's *governing activity*? Does this mean that everything that happens is a sign of God's micromanaging the details of your life? Explain your answer.

5. What is the relationship between God's will and your will?

6. On the top-ten list of God's will, name two or three of your favorites. Which ones are harder for you to follow?

## Moving On...

If you are anxious to get some guidance about some specific things in your life, such as your career, your finances, and your relationships, then all you have to do is turn the page. In the next chapter we're going to tell you how following the basic principles for knowing God's will can help you with the everyday choices in your life.

# Chapter 12

Where God has put a period, do not change
it to a question mark.

*T. J. Back*

In chapter 11, we gave you some plain and simple principles about the theology of God's will. But most Christians are more interested in knowing the specifics of God's plan rather than the theory behind it all. You probably want to know about God's will for your own life because you have some decisions to make. Perhaps...

- You are waiting for God to give you some sort of sign to guide you (celestial skywriting would be nice—nothing fancy—something in a Times New Roman font would be sufficient).

- You are jealous of all of your other Christian friends who seem to know exactly what God wants them to do with their lives.

- Your anxiety over finding God's will is ruining your enjoyment of God's love.

God isn't likely to put road signs along your morning commute route that reveal His will. So you probably won't see a billboard that says: "I've heard your prayers. The answers are *yes* to the job change, *wait* on the marriage proposal, and buy the *midnight blue* Camry." But don't be frustrated because God hasn't been giving you clear signals about choices in your life. In fact, get ready to say goodbye to your frustrations because God isn't trying to hide His will from you. He has made it pretty easy to find. You just have to know what you're looking for.

# How Do You Find God's Will?

You have spent your entire life playing guessing games. It started when you were an infant and your parents pestered you with that annoying "peek-a-boo" game. As a toddler, you were humiliated with the "guess which hand is holding the candy" game. By the time you were in elementary school, you suffered the indignity of searching for your older siblings in a game of "hide-and-seek," only to learn that they ditched you while you were counting to 100. Now you are much older, and the guessing still continues, whether it involves picking stocks on the NASDAQ or trying to find a missing sock that's not in the dryer.

Admit it. These guessing games have always frustrated you, but they seem to be a part of life. But when it comes to finding God's will, you thought you'd get a break because He would reveal it to you. But He hasn't, and you're stuck guessing at it.

## God Isn't Hiding, and Neither Is His Will

We've got good news for you. God doesn't like to play games. God doesn't try to hide from people. He has promised that He will reveal Himself to you if you are looking for Him.

> *"If you look for me in earnest, you will find me when you seek me. I will be found by you," says the* LORD (Jeremiah 29:13-14).

God even makes His existence obvious to people who aren't necessarily looking for Him.

> *From the time the world was created, people have seen the earth and sky and all that God made. They can clearly see his invisible qualities—his eternal power and divine nature. So they have no excuse whatsoever for not knowing God* (Romans 1:20).

Just as God makes Himself conspicuous (it is hard to hide when you are omnipresent), He takes the same approach with revealing His will. He isn't hiding it. Actually, He is anxious for you to find it.

### But You've Got to Know What You Are Looking For

Let's get one thing straight: God has a will for your life. That fact is obvious from verses like these:

> *We ask God to give you a complete understanding of what he wants to do in your lives* (Colossians 1:9).

> *Teach me to do your will, for you are my God* (Psalm 143:10).

> *Don't act thoughtlessly, but try to understand what the Lord wants you to do* (Ephesians 5:17).

So, if God has a will for your life, and if He wants you to know it, then why do so many Christians have a hard time finding it? Well, it just may be that they are looking for the wrong thing. Maybe you and God have different ideas of what His will looks like.

Maybe God's will is sitting right in front of you, but you aren't recognizing it.

Let's analyze God's will to see what we are talking about. It seems to break down into three different components: a sovereign plan for the universe, a moral code for all of humanity, and a general plan for your life.

### God's Sovereign Plan

God has a plan for the universe. Before He created the world, He planned exactly how things were going to go. It was more than just knowing in advance how random events were going to turn out. As we discussed in the last chapter, God is in control, and all events operate within the context of His exact plan. The result will be what He has intended all along.

For the most part, God's sovereign plan is hidden and unknown to us. Oh sure, we know a little bit about it because we can learn from what has happened in the past, and the Bible tells us a little bit about what is going to happen in the future. (What a convenient opportunity to put in a shameless plug for *Knowing the Bible 101* in our Christianity 101 series.) God doesn't expect us to understand—or even "find"—His sovereign plan. We just need to know that He has one and that He is in control (Romans 11:33-36).

### God's Moral Code

Another aspect of God's will includes the moral code that He has established for all of humanity. This moral code is simply God's standard of behavior and conduct, which is set forth in the Bible. We aren't talking about a set of do's and don'ts that must be strictly followed. God's moral code is mostly about principles that are beneficial for you. Things like "love your neighbor" and "always be thankful."

God expects us to know the principles of His moral code. You won't have any trouble finding them. They are in the Bible. It is just a matter of *reading* them and then *obeying* them. We shouldn't consider it a hardship to follow these general principles because we will be much better off if we do.

*Obey all the laws Moses gave you. Do not turn away from them, and you will be successful in everything you do. Study this Book of the Law continually. Meditate on it day and night so you may be sure to obey all that is written in it. Only then will you succeed* (Joshua 1:7-8).

## God's General Will for Your Life

Here we go. Now things are becoming very interesting because it is getting to be all about *you*. We know you are giddy with anticipation for us to reveal to you God's will for your life. And we are going to do it—we promise. But first, we need to refresh your memory a bit. (We know that in the excitement of discovering God's will at long last, you might have forgotten a few principles from the last chapter.)

- God wants you to believe in Jesus and accept Him as your Savior (John 3:16; 2 Peter 3:9).

- God wants you to be like Jesus (1 John 2:6).

- God wants you to know Him better and to submit to Him (Colossians 1:9-10; Micah 6:8).

Within those parameters of what God wants, we can boldly and confidently pronounce God's will for your life. Are you ready? Drum roll, please.

*It is God's will for your life that you have a growing relationship with Him that makes you more like Christ each day.*

Are you feeling cheated? You were probably expecting some specifics. We will get to the specifics of your life in just a moment. But for now, we are talking about God's general will for your life. It is not difficult to figure out God's will for you. It is simply knowing what He wants from you. As we set forth at the end of the last chapter and briefly summarized above, God wants a relationship with you and He wants you to be engaged in the process of becoming more Christlike. It is as simple as that. That is God's will for you.

God's will is not about a place or a thing or a time. God's will is all about the condition of your heart. That's what God really cares about. We overlook that fact when we trivialize God's will by thinking that it primarily applies to choosing between Coke or Pepsi, boxers or briefs, and decisions relating to whether you should wear the blue shirt or the green shirt.

- God's will is more about your *character* than it is about making *choices*.

- God's will is more about your *attitude* than it is about finding *answers*.

- God's will is more about your *relationship* with God than it is about getting *results*.

### And Now for the Specifics

We promised you that we would get to the specifics, and now we will. After all, we know that you have specific questions, and you need to make some specific decisions. There may be issues in your life that involve your family, your friendships, your education, your career, or your finances. They may be somewhat mundane (Should I buy or lease my next car?), or they may be monumental (Is this the person I should marry?).

Since you are interested in specific direction from God, you were probably disappointed when we explained that God's will for you is about your relationship with Him rather than results. Don't despair. As your relationship with God grows deeper, you will begin to think like He does. That new way of thinking will help you make decisions about the specific issues you are facing.

## What God's Will Is All About

Notice again the three components of God's will:

1. God's sovereign plan for the universe,

2. God's moral code for humanity, and

3. God's general will for you.

Notice that God doesn't have a specific, explicit, and detailed will for your life that involves your choices on everything from breakfast cereals to colleges. In some respects, that may make your life a little more difficult because many decisions are left up to your. On the other hand, you have freedom to make decisions within a wide range options (limited only by the parameters of God's moral code).

### What God's Will Is Not

We know you might be a bit disappointed to learn that God does not have a specific will for every issue in your life. Perhaps you were frustrated because you couldn't make decisions in your life, and you wanted God to provide the answers. Maybe your anxiety wasn't caused by your inability to choose; maybe you were just afraid that there was only one correct choice within God's will, and you didn't want to blow it.

Unfortunately, many people mistakenly believe that God's will is always very specific and limited to a single choice. That erroneous viewpoint misrepresents God's will. If you think that there is only one correct choice to any decision, then you will mistakenly view God's will as one of these:

- *A tightrope.* You have to walk carefully along God's will. You can't move too quickly, and all of your mental energy is focused on using that long pole to maintain your balance.

- *A maze.* Your life is a series of dead ends and wrong turns. You can't go very far in life without being confronted with a choice of turning left or right.

- *A bean under a cup.* You're fairly sure that you know where God's will is, but your guess is invariably wrong. You feel like a big loser (and you are sure that you hear God snickering).

Fortunately for us, God doesn't take sadistic pleasure in watching us sweat through the process of finding His will.

### God's Will Is About Guidance, Not Guessing

God's will is not some narrow tightrope, and we don't have to guess about it. Rather, it is all about the freedom to make choices within certain broad parameters. Those boundaries are His moral code. As long as our decisions do not violate scriptural principles, we are free to make whatever choice seems best to us. There may be many acceptable answers, and we don't need to worry that our decision will derail us from God's only preferred route.

When you think about it, the freedom God gives to us to make any choice within the bounds of His moral code is consistent with God's role. The Bible describes God as our King, our Father, and our Shepherd. Using those analogies, it is natural to expect that we would be given some decision-making freedom.

- *God as our King.* An evil dictator oppresses the citizens and gives them little freedom. They are told where to go and what to do. In contrast, a good king gives his subjects much freedom. While there may be rules in the kingdom for the beneficial functioning of the community, each subject can enjoy life without oppression.

- *God as our Father.* It is the goal of every father to raise his children to maturity. He doesn't want them to stay at an immature stage in which their every move must be watched. Part of the teaching process includes giving the child the freedom to make mistakes. With increasing maturity comes additional freedom. Eventually, the children will become wise enough to make decisions on their own.

- *God as our Shepherd.* The shepherd is responsible for making sure that the sheep have food to eat. How does that happen? The shepherd leads them to a field. Within the boundaries of that field, the sheep move around. They eat where they want. The shepherd doesn't point out each edible blade of grass.

We don't want to push these analogies too far. But you can see that God's moral code is similar to a king's laws, a curfew imposed by a father, or a pasture fence (maybe a comparison to a sheep dog is stretching it). As long as we are operating within those parameters, we enjoy the freedom to make choices, and any such choice is acceptable to God.

### God's Will Is a Circle, Not a Dot

In his book *Decision Making and the Will of God,* Garry Friesen uses the images of a circle and a dot to illustrate God's will. He uses a circle to represent God's moral code. Operating outside of the circle means that you are outside of God's will. But all decisions that fall within the circumference of the circle are acceptable to God (because they are within His moral code).

The premise of Friesen's book is that many people mistakenly believe that God has a limited, specific will for most of life's decisions. He uses a dot to illustrate this viewpoint. As he diagrams it, Friesen puts a dot in the center of the circle to represent the approach, which assumes that God has a specific will for every issue.

Friesen rejects the notion that we should be looking for a "dot" of God's will in each decision. Here is how he explains it:

> Scripture indicates that an area of freedom where genuine opportunity of choice is granted to the believer should replace the dot. For God's children, all things within the moral will of God are lawful, clean and pure. In decisions that are made within that moral will, the Christian should not feel guilty about his choice; neither should he fear that his decision is unacceptable to God. God has made it clear what He wants: His plan for His children is for them to enjoy the freedom that He has granted. It is a freedom that is clearly established in Scripture from the nature of laws, the nature of sin, and direct statements of the Bible.

Here is the bottom line: Stop searching for God's will as if it were a tiny dot. Dots are difficult to find, and God isn't trying to make His will like a buried treasure. Think of God's will as a circle in which you are free to make decisions. The more you develop your relationship with God, the easier it will be for you to make those decisions because you'll be approaching them from God's perspective.

## Three Things to Do Each Day

Each day of your life is filled with choices and decisions. Some decisions you make automatically (like brushing your teeth), while others take more time and thought (like starting a new business). You may not see the results of your more thoughtful decisions for days, months, or even years, but at some point the consequences of what you decide at any given moment are played out. People are affected, events are impacted, and circumstances are set into motion.

In addition to His sovereign plan for the universe and His moral code for humanity, God does have an "everyday will" for you. His everyday will probably doesn't involve the kind of toothpaste you use, but it would relate to those decisions about your new business. He cares about each decision you make to establish your business and build it into a success. God wants your everyday decisions to line up with His everyday will for you. You get to decide, but God wants you to focus on Him each step of the way. Here are three things you can do to keep all your decisions in the context of God's will:

### 1. Commit to Do the Will of God

Do you want to find God's will in a particular situation? Then don't play "Let's Make a Deal" with God. Don't say to God, "Tell me what Your will is, and then I'll decide if I want to do it or not." God doesn't play that game, so don't play that game with God. In his little book, *How to Know the Will of God,* Russ Johnston wrote, "God does not reveal His will to curiosity seekers." If you're curious rather than serious about God's everyday will for you, you'll never know what it is.

Committing to the will of God involves trusting God. You have to trust that God has your best interests in mind at all times. He knows you better than you know yourself, and He knows what's best for you. God knows your weaknesses, and He knows your strengths. God knows your fears, and He knows your hopes. God will never mislead you or do you harm.

Trusting God for your future—whether that future is tomorrow or ten years from now—begins with trusting God now. And you don't have to wait long for the payoff. Once you have committed to do God's will—regardless of what it is—God will show you what it is step-by-step.

> *Trust in the LORD with all your heart; do not depend on your own understanding. Seek his will in all you do, and he will direct your paths* (Proverbs 3:5-6).

## 2. See Things from God's Perspective

You know how important it is to get a bird's-eye view of things. Before you explore New York at ground level, it's important to study a map so you can find your way around. Before you decide to major in quantum physics, you need to read the course descriptions so you can determine if your strengths fit the requirements. The same principle applies to God's everyday will: You need to get a "God's-eye view" before you can do it.

This is going to sound a little contradictory, but hear us out. When you insist on doing God's will from *your* perspective, then your main concern is *doing*. You get caught up on your own performance. By contrast, when you do God's will from *His* perspective, you are more concerned about *being*. God wants you to do stuff for Him, but He's more interested in the kind of person you are becoming than the specific thing you are doing. He knows that when your *being* is right, then your *doing* will be right. And when your *doing* is right, then God gets the credit He deserves, no matter what it is you're doing.

> *Whatever you eat or drink or whatever you do, you must do all for the glory of God* (1 Corinthians 10:31).

## 3. Let God Work in You

The final thing God wants you to know before you do His everyday will is that you don't have to do it all by yourself. God has promised to help you.

*For God is working in you, giving you the desire to obey*
*him and the power to do what pleases him* (Philippians
2:13).

What would you do if Bill Gates came to you and said, "I
believe in you so much that I'm going to put all of my wealth and
power at your disposal to help you succeed"? Would you accept
Bill's offer (even if you don't do Windows)? Of course you would!

So here's God (whose wealth and power make Mr. Gates'
resources look like a pimple on an elephant's backside), and He's
saying, "I believe in you so much that I'm going to put all of my
resources at your disposal to help you succeed." Should you
accept God's offer? Absolutely!

*I pray that from his glorious, unlimited resources he will*
*give you mighty inner strength through his Holy Spirit. And*
*I pray that Christ will be more and more at home in your*
*hearts as you trust in him* (Ephesians 3:16-17).

## Five Resources God Has for You

Make no mistake about it. Making wise decisions in the context of God's will isn't easy. Often it's complicated. Sometimes it's
frustrating. But just like anything worth doing, God's will is
always rewarding. Even if you aren't certain about what your
next move should be, you can trust God that He will never lead
you astray. God may not reveal His everyday will when you
think you need it, but He will show you when He knows you need
it. Be patient. Wait for God's perfect timing.

Having said that, you don't have to sit around wondering
what to do next. Waiting for God's timing doesn't mean that you
do nothing. You have the freedom to use your thoughtful judgment, your previous experience, and your current research to
make wise decisions in the context of God's will.

You also have the freedom to bring God into the decision-
making process at each step. Does this mean you should look
into the sky, ask God for advice, and then listen for Him to
respond each time you need to make a decision? Well, there are
worse things you could do, but we were thinking along more

practical lines. Remember, God's will is more about guidance than guessing. God isn't a fortune-teller, and neither is He a divine dictator. God is your Guide, and He has given to you certain resources that you'll need to help you make wise decisions in the context of His will for your life. Here are the five resources that God has given to you:

# Look in Your Bag

You may not use all of these God-centered resources each time you are faced with a decision, but you need to get really good at using all of them. Think of your life as a golf course, and you're a golfer. You aren't going to use each club in your bag on every hole, but you need to be ready to use each club when the shot requires it. Just as you need to know what clubs are in your bag, you need to know the resources that God provides for knowing His will.

### 1. The Word of God

Most of God's everyday will for you is contained in His Word, the Bible, and that's because the Bible is God's personal message for you. This is the way God talks to you. People who don't know God's Word don't know God's will. They don't know the essential things God wants for them because they don't read the Bible regularly, and they don't study it systematically. Don't make this mistake. The Word of God is your primary source of guidance.

> *Your word is a lamp for my feet and a light for my path* (Psalm 119:105).

The Bible contains many direct principles, which Chuck Swindoll calls, "specific, black-and-white truths that take all the guesswork out of the way." Here's an example:

> *Let there be no sexual immorality, impurity, or greed among you. Such sins have no place among God's people.*

*Obscene stories, foolish talk, and coarse jokes—these are not for you* (Ephesians 5:3).

There's no gray area there, and the Bible is full of such specifics. If you are doing anything that contradicts these principles, then you can be sure you are out of the will of God. And even if the Bible doesn't give you a black-and-white answer about something you are going to encounter, you'll find plenty of general guidelines to help you navigate through the gray areas of your life. Here's an example:

*For though your hearts were once full of darkness, now you are full of light from the Lord, and your behavior should show it! For this light within you produces only what is good and right and true* (Ephesians 5:8-9).

Finding and following God's will requires spiritual maturity and good judgment, which come when you know God's Word.

---

*H*as it ever struck you that the vast majority of the will of God for your life has already been revealed in the Bible? That is a crucial thing to grasp.

*Paul Little*

---

## 2. Talking with God

If God talks to you through the Bible, then the way you talk with God is through prayer. King David wrote, "The LORD will answer when I call to him" (Psalm 4:3). "Devote yourselves to prayer," wrote the apostle Paul (Colossians 4:2). And Jesus, who knew more about prayer than anyone else, said, "Keep on asking, and you will be given what you ask for" (Matthew 7:7).

Do you wonder what you should do in a particular situation? Pray to God about it. Ask Him for an answer. But realize this: If you want to know God's will for you, you need to pray according to His will.

*And we can be confident that he will listen to us whenever we ask him for anything in line with his will* (1 John 5:14)

This isn't a circular argument. This doesn't mean that you need to know God's will for a particular situation before you ask God to reveal His will to you. Praying according to God's will means praying according to Scripture. It means you will never ask God for something you know is contradictory to His nature or His Word. Praying according to God's will also means praying with faith, trusting that God has your best interest in mind at all times.

> *The earnest prayer of a righteous person has great power and wonderful results* (James 5:16).

### 3. The Spirit of God

When it comes to knowing and doing God's will, the Holy Spirit is your secret weapon. He's the inside source "who leads into all truth" (John 14:17). Sometimes the word "prompting" is used to describe the Holy Spirit's work in your life. Here's what it means. Think of "prompting" in the sense of "control," because when you let the Holy Spirit control you (Ephesians 5:18), then you are giving your whole life over to God, so that whatever you do, you are doing it in the will of God and to the glory of God (1 Corinthians 10:31). If you are walking in the light by reading your Bible, and you are talking with God through prayer, then you are also in the Holy Spirit's control, and your inner promptings are more likely to be God speaking to you.

The Holy Spirit can also provide you with the "peace of God," which is an inner assurance that the big decision you just made was the correct one (even though it will bring about major changes and consequences). If you find your stomach in knots, then you might be leaning the wrong way in your decision-making process, but if your stomach feels fine and you have peace in your heart, then your decision is probably a good one. (Note: Don't confuse the work of the Holy Spirit with the natural gastronomic disruptions caused by indulging in three chili burgers and a quart of Pepsi.)

### 4. The Work of God

At any given moment, you are connected to a variety of people, places, and events, and these things are constantly changing. Your life is fluid, not stationary. If you want to know

God's will for you today, you need to be aware of what's going on around you. "Look around you!" Jesus told His disciples. "Vast fields are ripening all around us and are ready now for the harvest" (John 4:35). As someone who is eager to do God's will, you need to open your eyes today and see where God is working.

Bible teacher Henry Blackaby writes about the "momentum" of God's will. It is likely that God will want you involved with something He is already doing. Notice where God seems to be at work in the activities around you, because it is possible that He wants you to join in. The best place to start looking is in the ministries of the church that you are attending.

## 5. The People of God

You may be in the Word, your prayer life may be in excellent shape, and you may feel as though the Holy Spirit is prompting you to do something—but you're still not absolutely sure. Are you lacking faith? Not necessarily. More likely, you need a little more confirmation. That's where the wise counsel of other Christians comes into play. King Solomon, the wisest man who ever lived, didn't rely on his superior judgment and intellect alone. He sought out trusted advisers.

> *Plans go wrong for a lack of advice; many counselors bring success* (Proverbs 15:22).

God doesn't expect you to make big decisions on your own. He has put people around you—your family, your friends, your pastor, and other members of your church—who are spiritually equipped to help you see God's will clearly. Ultimately the decision to follow God's will is yours, but remember that God uses other Christians to help you know what His will is.

## How's That for a Cohesive Conclusion?

We think this list of five resources that God has made available to you to discover and follow His will makes an excellent conclusion for this book. In the previous 11 chapters we have reviewed the things you should be doing to grow in your faith as a Christian. God hasn't given those assignments to you as busywork or to keep you occupied so you won't have time for sinning.

The things we've previously outlined are the activities of a growing Christian who is intent on knowing God's will for his or her life. Don't do these things out of a sense of obligation. Do them because you want to know God better and follow His will for your life.

# What's That Again?

1. God has a sovereign plan for the universe, a moral code for humanity, and a general will for your life.

2. God's general will for your life is that you have a growing relationship with Him, which makes you more like Christ each day. God's everyday will for your life may involve some specific decisions and directions, but His will is focused more on *who* you are than *where* you go or *what* you do.

3. God's will is not a tightrope, a maze, or a bean under a cup. Think of God's will more as a circle than as a dot. You've got a lot of freedom in making choices so long as you stay within His moral code.

4. There are three things you can do to keep your decisions in the context of God's will: commit to do the will of God, see things from God's perspective, and let God work in you.

5. God may not reveal His will when you think you need it, but He will clearly reveal it when He knows you need it.

6. God has given you the resources you need to make wise decisions in the context of His will for your life. These are the Word of God, talking with God, the Holy Spirit, the ongoing work of God, and the people of God.

## Dig Deeper

We're always fascinated by the subject of knowing God's will. And we've enjoyed reading these books on the topic:

> *The Mystery of God's Will* by Charles R. Swindoll. Here you'll find an explanation that God's will is not so much a destination as much as it is a journey.

> *Decision Making and the Will of God* by Garry Friesen. This book does a great job of explaining the circle-dot analogy and revealing some of the misconceptions about God's will.

> *The Fight* by John White. This book discusses the practical aspects of Christian living. The chapter entitled "guidance" has an excellent discussion of God's will.

---

# $\mathcal{Q}$uestions for $\mathcal{R}$eflection and $\mathcal{D}$iscussion

1. Why do many Christians (maybe even you) think that knowing God's will is so difficult?

2. Explain the analogies of the tightrope and the maze. Why aren't these accurate depictions of God's will?

3. Describe the meaning of God's sovereign plan for the universe, God's moral code for humanity, and God's general will for you.

4. Explain the circle-dot thing. Give some examples.

5. Review the five resources that God uses to help you discover His will. Do you find one resource more helpful than others? Is there one which you have ignored in the past?

6. Get personal and think of several examples in the past when you were seeking God's will for a decision you were facing. Did you know what you were looking for? Is there anything in this chapter that might have changed your approach?

7. Now get really personal. What are the "God's will" issues that you are dealing with right now? How are you going to approach ascertaining God's will on these matters?

## Moving On...

We've got one word of caution before we leave you. Don't make the mistake of thinking that we've given to you a holy checklist of the things you need to do in order to qualify as a "good Christian." God isn't really into rules and regulations and checklists. God cares more about your real life than a forced religious life. As a Christian, your real life should be all about your relationship with God.

Don't look at the subjects of this book (including reading the Bible, praying, witnessing, and going to church) as your mandatory Christian To Do list. Of course, these are things that you should do, and you should do them even when you don't feel like it. But God isn't going to love you more because you do them (just like He won't love you less if you skip doing them). Your motivation to do these things should be all about Jesus. That is the way that you are going to know Him better and deepen your relationship with Him. And that is what growing as a Christian is all about.

# Index

The authors would enjoy hearing from you.
The best ways to contact them are
Twelve Two Media
P.O. Box 25997
Fresno, CA 93729

**E-mail**
info@twelvetwomedia.com

**Website**
www.twelvetwomedia.com

## *Exclusive Online Feature*
Here's a study feature you're really going to like!
Simply go online at

### www.christianity101online.com

There you will find a website designed exclusively for readers of *Growing as a Christian 101* and other books and Bible studies in the Christianity 101 series. When you log on to the site, just click on the book you are studying, and you will discover additional information, resources, and helps, including

- *Background Material*—We can't put everything in this book, so this online section includes more material, such as historical, geographical, theological, and biographical information.

- *More Questions*—Do you need more questions for your group study? Here are additional questions for each chapter. Bible study leaders will find this especially helpful.

- *Answers to Your Questions*—Do you have a question about something you read in this book? Post your question and an "online scholar" will respond.

- *FAQs*—In this section are answers to some of the most frequently asked questions about the topic you are studying.

What are you waiting for? Go online and become a part of the Christianity 101 community!

# Christianity 101® Series

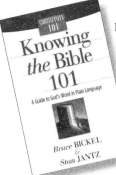

### Knowing the Bible 101
Enrich your interaction with Scripture with this user-friendly guide, which shows you the Bible's story line and how each book fits into the whole. Learn about the Bible's themes, terms, and culture, and find out how you can apply the truths of every book of the Bible to your own life.

### Creation & Evolution 101
With their distinctively winsome style, Bruce Bickel and Stan Jantz explore the essentials of creation and evolution and offer fascinating evidence of God's hand at work. Perfect for individual or group use.

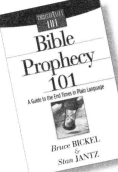

### Bible Prophecy 101
In their contemporary, down-to-earth way, Bruce and Stan present the Bible's answers to your end-times questions. You will appreciate their helpful explanations of the rapture, the tribulation, the millen-- nium, Christ's second coming, and other important topics.

### Knowing God 101
This book is brimming with joy! What-- ever your background, you will love the inspiring descriptions of God's nature, personality, and activities. You will also find straightforward responses to the essential questions about God.

### Growing as a Christian 101
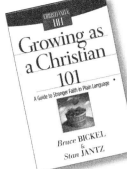
In this fresh new look at the essentials of the Christian walk, Bruce Bickel and Stan Jantz offer readers the encouragement they need to continue making steady progress in their spiritual lives.